Touching Your Heart

Touching Your Heart

LYRA F. NORONHA

PARTRIDGE
A Penguin Random House Company

To order additional copies of this book, contact
Partridge India
000 800 10062 62
orders.india@partridgepublishing.com

www.partridgepublishing.com/india

To my father, the late Charles Noronha,
and
my mother, Amy Noronha,

my rocks and
the reason I am who I am.

Acknowledgements

I cannot go ahead without thanking my immediate family, relatives, and friends for all their love, support, and encouragement; for their belief in me; and for the support I have received from all of them in many ways all these years. Thanks for being there for me and for putting up with me.

I also wish to thank Tehruna Patel, Alison Aranha, Sharon Mascarenhas, and Uday Gupta for reviewing my several drafts and giving me tips that prodded this book along.

I could not have completed this book without acknowledging all my patients and their families, relatives, and friends whom I have encountered in my tenure. You have been the reason I am a nurse, and it is your story that I narrate.

Lastly, I would like to acknowledge all my nurse colleagues and counterparts, teachers, professors, directors, and all the other medical and paramedical colleagues who have been part of my life. I treasure each and every one of you for making every hospital shift I worked memorable. Thanks for being there for me, for helping me stick it out with you. We are one big family. Thanks.

Foreword

The content of this book is rather interesting to the lay-person. As the author so often points out in her book, the **Medical Faculty** are, after all, humans and do encounter moments of horror, sadness, compassion, hurt and joy which are kept well hidden from the patients and their families, in order to give them confidence, while maintaining an appearance of professionalism.

As the Title -*"TOUCHING YOUR HEART"* suggests, the author has been able to put forth her memoirs, the hardships and the joys, the disappointments and the achievements, the humane indelible moments that touched her soul .... all represented with deep honesty and great simplicity. The fluidity of the book is good and interestingly she has started each topic with an apt quote, keeping the descriptions short and captivating, in a narrative that is simple, infused with a colloquial flavor.... making the book an easy but insightful read.

TEHRUNA PATEL

Contents

Work is love made visible. It is to sow seeds
with tenderness and reap the harvest with joy
even as if your beloved were to eat the fruit.

Khalil Gibran

Introduction

The realization came to me suddenly one lonely evening. Life had thrown many unexpected twists my way. I was looking for answers which would bring comfort to my troubled spirit. I was at the seashore one early evening at a time when the sun was just hiding away for the night. The sky was painted with a light peachy hue. There was a slight breeze in the air, and it brought along with it what I was looking for. The answer which I received was something I could not ignore any more. So after staring at the ocean for a very long time, I proceeded to head home armed with my answer. I took out my diary and revisited all my earlier writings. Over the years, my random scribbles after a hard day at work were given a look-over. This is how you have in your hands what I started on that day. This is the birth of my stories.

Hospitals are a strange place to spend your whole life in. For the medical fraternity, this is our home. This is a place that you dread going to, a place that you fear, but we are very comfortable living in it. This is our home away from home. While others work at a desk, buried in files, goals, targets, and deadlines, we work with life itself. We are present at the exhibition of the 'life art'.

When I was in nursing school, I was taught anatomy, physiology, surgery, and psychiatry. I learnt and devoured all these subjects with zeal and diligence. During our studentship, we got to learn these subjects very objectively, yet not one of our professors prepared us for the lessons in life we were about to encounter on —happiness, joy, pain, agony, and sorrow, a storm of emotions displayed many times over, and the mystery of life and death all occurring within the same time frame, sometimes a breadth's distance from each other.

Initially, it was overwhelming for me to absorb all this. I was young, an eighteen-year-old, when I got myself admitted into nursing school, and within six months, I had to make my first visit to the hospitals. My very first patient contact was at the most at the age of nineteen. I cannot remember all the faces; some are just a blur, but the experiences are forever etched in my memory. Every now and then, the memories resurface, rekindled by a spark of circumstance that I face every day.

Life's many facets and the myriad colours of life's canvas draw you unwillingly. The medical field propels you into an emotional growth spurt and takes you on a roller-coaster ride to appreciate life and living. I have experienced so much out there that I do not think anything or anyone can shock me any more.

Initially, I wrote the book as a catharsis for myself. It was my de-stresser. It was much later that I sat and sifted through all my musings. It was my way to reflect on the day's work. The more I thought about it, the stronger my conviction got to share this with the world, to paint for the world what hospitals look from within.

These stories are true incidents, and it is a compilation over the years of events that I have experienced and would like to share with you so that you can experience the same of what I have experienced. These events or stories—call it what you like—are all direct encounters. The stories have warmed my heart, touched the depths of my soul, and I wish that they warm your hearts too. The love and human spirit are there for everyone to see, smell, and touch. I do not wish you to be disturbed by reading some of what I have written as that is not my intention.

Rather, my objective is to awaken you to life and living. I have also very intentionally not mentioned names, religions, and nationalities. I wish you to be drawn to rich human emotions and experiences and not to any particular facet of our circumstances. I wish not to influence you with any preconceived prejudice towards any person or group. Talking about influencing you, I have not added any melodrama to spice up the book; none of the stories in this book are a figment of my imagination.

A warning though before you embark on this journey with me: I guess this book is not for the faint-hearted as it would definitely make you cringe in disbelief and horror at times. Yet true it is, and I give it to you as it is. It is a first-hand encounter of moments of absolute awe. And all these events have taught me invaluable lessons.

Part I

It All Started with 'Why Did I Become a Nurse?'

I slept and dreamt that life was a joy.
I awoke and saw that life was a service.
I acted and behold, service was a joy.

Rabindranath Tagore

I cannot pinpoint the exact answer to that question, but I do remember that I was in the eighth standard, roughly about thirteen years old when the thought came: 'You have to become a nurse.' Looking back, I believe it was a calling for me. I was chosen for the profession.

Now I had no relatives or friends who were nurses, so I had no first-hand role models for motivation or inspiration. If I recall the earliest memory of a nurse for me, it was portrayed by the Bollywood actress Meena Kumari in the romantic saga *Dil Apna Preet Parai*. The thought of becoming a nurse somehow became very strong, and it caught on me. The period then was the late seventies. As much as I tried to, I could not push the thought away.

I can remember the very moment that I told my parents about my desire to become a nurse. My mum, though not highly educated, was aware by then about the graduate nursing programme. She insisted that I enrol only for a bachelor's degree in nursing, and thus I ventured on this path. It was a path of growth, knowledge, and understanding not so much of the textbooks, but more about life and its challenges. It was a path of feeling someone else's pain and partaking of someone else's joy, a journey of healing and helping not just the lives of all whom I come into contact with but also my very own life in the process.

In the years that passed, I did ask my colleagues why they joined nursing. For most of them, the reason for their initiation into nursing remains varied, such as financial and security reasons. Yet the reason why they continue to stay in nursing is the same—the caring nature of the task brings solace to their hearts.

Embarking on a Journey

The journey of a thousand miles
begins with one step.

Lao Tzu

My first recollection of being a nurse was actually wearing the nurse's uniform with all its trimmings. I still remember trying to fix this cap with multiple bobby pins in my hair. The cap was always my nightmare, and I could never mould it to fit my head. It was absolutely unyielding in nature like a stubborn mule which refuses to go your way, and I was very often frustrated with it. I am sure a lot of nurses thought of it as their crowning glory, but never once did I perceive it in that way.

Having great difficulty to starch the cap stiff, we never ventured to wash it. We wore it for months at a time once it was starched stiff like a *"paper masala dosa" which is a south Indian food delicacy*. The cap has been part of the uniform during the times of Florence Nightingale. In those days, it was designed like a huge envelope on top of the head to hold all the hair together. Slowly, that trend changed, and the cap became just a decorative piece atop the head. Eventually, the cap was removed as part of the uniform due to infection control reasons as it possibly caused more harm—though unintentional.

The stockings were something else altogether. Actually, at the time when I was a student nurse, they weren't even stockings; they were just knee-length socks that we had to wear with garters. If you are anything like me (that is, roly-poly), then a constant job is to pull the socks or stockings up as the garter keeps tumbling down, like Jack and Jill with the pail of water. In desperation, at times I would put huge thick rubber bands, which nearly threatened to stop the blood circulation in my lower limbs. Along with all the gory sights we had to see, I am surprised that I never once succumbed to a faint due to the pooling of blood in my lower half.

The rest of the get-up, I cannot say much about, but it sort of completed the look. The super-white nursing uniform—I wonder why it never surfaced in any washing powder advert till now—has come a long way since then. Different colours to soothe the patients are now worn, such as pastel blues and pinks, and the dreadful cap is done away with. There was a time we were strictly discouraged to put on the slightest hint of colour on our cheeks, but that concept has now changed.

Eventually, we were given the green signal to go ahead and don subtle colours on our faces. I remember one of my nursing directors instructing us not to look like our patients, with pale cheeks.

Nurse training involved strict discipline (akin to that in the military), yet it is because of that training that we became disciplined—waking up and sleeping at unearthly hours, wearing stiffly starched uniforms that hurt at the creases, and standing for hours on end without complaining about it. And if that was not enough, we had to deal with matronly, conservative senior nurses.

The downside of this profession is that we got used to highly erratic and irregular sleeping patterns as well as we had no regular mealtimes. Out of all this, some of us do suffer from the very ailments that we treat our patients for, such as diabetes and hypertension. Anxiety and stress are added to this mix as we are unable to focus on family issues since some of us do not get to spend time with our families. Celebrations and festive occasions are often given a miss.

I remember being a young girl just out of the twelfth standard and all of eighteen years old, trying to catch the first state public-transport bus. At that time, the first bus of the day, the number being 214, would come around six in the morning. I would wait by the window of our apartment and watch as the bus made its way on our street. Now the bus would wind its way up to the terminal stop and collect me on its way down as we lived by the second bus station. As the bus came into my vision, it would invariably mean an early morning sprint. In those days, I've never heard of any hundred-metre Olympic dash, made famous in recent times by Usain Bolt. This energy burst jump-started my early mornings. The bus plied along the railway station route, and that was where most of us got off. Then we got on to a train as our morning shift in the hospital would start at seven o'clock sharp.

As student nurses, we had to present ourselves even earlier as we had to line up for inspection. Remember that I said it was akin to the military. Even a five-minute delay or being shoddily dressed was not permitted, and we would be asked for a written explanation. Out of this, we became the most punctual at attendance. Yet no one monitored what time we ended our shift, and many a time, we would go home very late. Now a small minority of us did not stay in the hostel, and so we had to commute every day to and fro, which we accepted as our daily norm.

At that time, it was a female college degree, and not many male nurses enrolled into nursing. In fact, it was much later that I got introduced to the concept of male nurses. We became very independent and resilient as it was survival of the fittest, and we somehow had to fit into that category. When I mention *the fittest*, I focus on both physical and mental strengths as the job demanded high levels from both spheres. And we did this with no technology, no mobile, no Twitter, no chats, no Instagram, and none whatsoever of those present in today's modern-day electronic gadgets.

During my time as a student, each year was broken into six-month terms. We had to complete all disciplines of medicine, which I did make a mention of earlier. We spent hours poring over hard-copy textbooks in dimly lit libraries to push us through the semesters.

On the practical side, I still remember that the very first thing we had to master was bed-making. Trying to learn how to make mitred corners seemed to be so exciting at that time. It was a corner encountered during bed-making where you had to take the bed linen and tuck and flip at the same time. The bed-making had to be accomplished *with* or *without* the patient in bed. Each of us was given a list of nursing skill competencies for each semester. In the eighties, the behavioural competency element had not yet been conceptualized, and so we had to make do as we walked along this pathway on our own through trial and error.

Our nurse supervisor had to actually sign off that each one of us was competent in doing the required task. One of the most basic competencies was learning to give a sponge bath in bed to a patient who was not permitted bathroom privileges. Along with this, you could add patients who were supposed to be given a hair wash in bed. I could recollect that the hair wash was something else altogether. Have you ever tried to wash someone's hair while the person is in bed? It meant rolling a rubber mackintosh to end up in a bucket that was positioned below the head of the patient. Pouring warm water, lathering the patient's head, and ensuring that no puddle formed around your area needed skill, patience, and a patient who was willing to go through this for us.

We had to find patients every day for each of these nursing skill competencies. We could not force a patient to endure a sponge bath in bed when the patient could very well venture to do it themselves. Each one of us jostled for patients and the time from our nurse supervisor to supervise us so as to accomplish this long list of competencies. And as we completed the list, the bragging would start, especially to our contemporaries who did not yet complete the list. We started our student day with assigned patients. Additionally, we searched around for patients who were prescribed different physician orders, so that we could fulfil our long list of competency requirements laid down by our curriculum. Friends would help find patients suited for the completion of the list just in case we were nearing the end of our term and had not yet completed the list.

Strangely, in those days, we had to accomplish all this with no personal protective equipment, such as gloves, masks, or aprons. These resources were not readily available at our disposal. From those times, I also remember giving my first intramuscular injection. I was taught how to hold the injection and position it for entering the skin. We actually kept praying that our hands would not shake, that our supervisor would be lenient, and that we would be assigned to a kind patient. The greatest compliment was when our patients tell us that our hands were light and that they did not feel the injection at all.

As students, we were not permitted to administer intravenous injections, and I guess all nurses need to apologize to the scores of patients who were our guinea pigs while we learnt the art and skill of administering injections. I am sure not one of us nurses will be able to tell you that we managed to get it right on the first attempt of our intravenous injection. We never disclosed to our patients while injecting them that it was our first attempt at administering an intravenous (IV) injection. Doing it on a mannequin is completely different from administering it in a real-life situation to a patient. As we saw the drop of blood coming through the syringe when we pulled the piston, we heaved a huge sigh of relief that we had hit the vein. In those days, the privilege of disposable syringes and needles was not available. So we had to make do with glass syringes and had to manually re-sterilize the syringe and needle for reuse.

The best moment at that time for me was anxiously waiting to witness a birth of life—the cry of the newborn as the baby gulps air, the cut that we make on the pulsating but slippery umbilical cord, recognizing our own births, and the newfound respect we had for our own mothers in witnessing the pain that each mother endures. It was a miracle unfolding in front of you, and after that, the only thing that could match it was bathing those absolute bundles of joy. We used to jostle with one another to bathe the newborn babies; it was the most pleasant times we had.

We had one rural posting included in our public health posting. This entailed a group of us staying together for, I think, a period of three months. For some of us, this was the first time we were away from our parents, and this in itself was difficult. But we also learnt how difficult rural life was as we had to adopt three families for that time period and follow their health issues and challenges that plague them. In this time, we also had to build a trusting relationship with the families. These families would allow us inside their humble houses and actually open up and tell us their problems. Do not forget we were all of about twenty-one years old at that time, and this was an eye-opener.

I remember we did a leprosy awareness and diagnostic drive into the slums for a whole day in health promotion. That day was hot, exhausting, sweaty, and dirty, but we got an insight into how others who are less privileged than us live. We also had to participate in blood donation drives, which meant we tried marketing blood donation to everyone around us whom we came into contact with. We were allowed to break into groups—the talkers and walkers—and marketed by going on to the streets, nearby colleges, and commercial institutions. Like I have said earlier, that was an era of no technology; everything had to be achieved manually. Nowadays, you can organize an event of any magnitude by the click of your fingers. I was introduced to donating blood from a young age as I had to practise what I preached.

I cannot think of any other profession that would have awakened all my senses in the way the Lady with the Lamp has done to me. It is a much-disciplined profession, and I will go on to say it is a calling, a dedication. I have to say that nurses are there round the clock with our patients; we take all the emotional pain, grief, and turmoil, and we package them with smiles and care in our hearts. We soothe the brow and heal with our touch. We do this not only for our patients but also attempt even to impart the same warmth to the family and relatives of our patients.

Like physicians, early on during our training in anatomy and physiology, we get to see dead bodies immersed in strongly concentrated solution of formaldehyde. These bodies were probably unclaimed or donated to medical science. The dead bodies were approximately six months old. My first such body had open eyes staring into space and was cut open multiple times, over and over again. It felt surreal, like it was not happening to me. That was when I knew that I could stomach this. I was made for this. I think some of us are chosen and fitted with a built-in courage so immense. With grit and determination, we forged along on this roller-coaster ride of human emotions.

Part II

My First Tears as a Nurse

Tears shed for self are tears of weakness, but
tears shed for others are a sign of strength.

Billy Graham

As a student nurse, we were assigned patients
with very basic clinical needs in our first six
to twelve months. So I was assigned this very portly
old lady who suffered from diabetes and who had
a huge abscess like a ravine on her back. I had to
assist one of the doctors, an intern at that time, to
do the dressing for the deep wound on her back. Not
much help I was because all the time I had to fight
back tears while holding this old mama's hands as
she cried out in pain. The doctor was probably doing
his job of getting rid of the infection, but as he was
digging into her wounds, my heart would miss a
heartbeat.

What made matters worse was that I was
positioned in front of the lady, holding her blouse
up to enable better visualization for the physician.
I was also trying to restrain mama so the physician
could have an unobstructed view and access to do
his job efficiently. The doctor was standing behind
the patient, so he was unable see mama's agony. But

I could see mama's pain, and I guess mama could see my discomfort. I was disturbed with what mama had to endure. It was also my very first introduction to *diabetes*, along with loads of pain both for me and mama, and to this day, I am not sure if I really helped that old mama or if, rather, she had helped me.

The Ugly Truth of Nursing

Nothing is so strong as gentleness,
nothing so gentle as real strength.

Saint Francis de Sales

I had worked in a rudimentary nursing home for a few weeks to acquire the required number of delivery cases during my student period. This nursing home was also a voluntary shelter for unwanted babies—no questions asked, anonymity guarded. It was by no means posh, and even the basic hospital facility and equipment that we take for granted in other organizations were scarce or just not there. If you ask me now to do what I did then, I would flatly refuse. But then, we were ignorant.

I have delivered babies with my bare hands in this nursing home—no gloves or protection; not that we knew the term *infection control* then. You see, I did not practise nursing in the prehistoric age but in the early eighties, and yet even then, we did not have all the facilities to provide safe care. We did not know the concept of hand hygiene, and yet after a delivery, I kept washing my hands time after time. Why, you may ask, did I wash my hands so religiously? Did I have the makings of someone with obsessive compulsive disorder?

Hey, did you ever smell amniotic fluid? It stank, period. Amniotic fluid is the fluid inside the uterus during pregnancy. And no matter how much I washed my hands, the smell of amniotic fluid would never go away. Eventually, we were immune to the smell and would proceed to eat straight after that. Babies were delivered left, right, and centre in this place—no ultrasounds or modern gadgets. Difficult deliveries were dealt with in a very crude, old-fashioned method, with nurses sitting astride the woman's belly and pushing away to glory towards the birth canal. Weeping pregnant mothers were scolded and abused in a vulgar way by these nurses who were delivering them.

Yes, I have said it. Since the day I have witnessed it, I have wanted to implore to the few who use this methodology to refrain from using it. At that time when it happened, I was too timid, too young, a student nurse, and could not—would not—voice my opinion. But now the truth is told, and it is the ugly truth of our so-called noble profession—that some of us can be rude and uncaring and become so immune to others' suffering and pain.

After Death

Our dead are never dead to us, until
we have forgotten them.

George Eliot

We were posted in one of biggest governmental hospitals. Through connections, we were permitted to view what not many would be allowed to watch—as well as not many would be able to stomach. We were scheduled to watch a postmortem. 'After death' is the actual meaning of *postmortem*. This procedure was an eye-opener for me, and maybe this was my turning point. The way I viewed life after that changed 360 degrees. I was about twenty-one years old, standing on the threshold of a life-changing moment, oblivious to what was to come down on me.

I was in my third year of nursing college. One of our classmates had connections with a physician who worked in a government hospital, and he arranged it so that a few from our batch who had the guts and all the digestive systems intact for it could view a postmortem. It was not like we had never seen dead bodies. By then, we had seen bodies that were used for dissections and for the study of anatomy and physiology. Very early on, as part of our nursing training, we did get to witness deaths of our patients, and we were not shielded from death as it would be part of our profession. Yet on the day that we were going for the postmortem, I do not think that any one of us was actually prepared for the real-life (not *reel*) theatre we had ringside tickets for.

We were taken into a dark hallway towards the mortuary, which is a euphemism for *dead house*. The smell, or rather the stench of death, mixed with the chemicals gave it away before we even entered the place. It was not part of our curriculum, and we went without our tutors, so we had no backup or emotional support. We were the bold lot of our batch, or so we thought of ourselves. I do not think that all nurses get to witness a postmortem, and I am not sure if I was fortunate to see one so early in life. I need to warn you before you proceed down the path that I will now take. Brace yourself for this story—that is all I am going to tell you. That day, we got no prior warning, or maybe we did get a warning in our heads, but we ignored it as we were too young or too obstinate to care.

As we entered this huge hall and our eyes fell on the dead bodies, we were silent; all our chatter and laughter instantly died down. All our carefree nature darkened, and we were in a sober mood. There must have been about six blocks in that huge hall. Each block was made up of grey stone or concrete material about eight to nine feet in breadth and about four feet in height. Naked adult bodies of mixed sexes, male and female, were lying on the blocks. And just that sight got me thinking about the purpose of life, and this is what it eventually all boils down to.

Unfortunately, there were no sheets to cover these bodies. I was not even sure about the identity of these bodies; they were presumably unclaimed bodies with no blood relatives but all waiting for a postmortem to be conducted on them. I cringed and felt naked myself, uncovered, and horribly uncomfortable. Yet I never left the room as I was embarrassed to leave and did not wish to admit that I was uncomfortable. So I was glued to the ground, waiting for the procedure to begin. I think each one of us wished not to be present at the postmortem, but not one of us had the initial courage to say it and leave the dreadful place.

I know that I am now going to get graphic, but I would like you to visualize what I as a twenty- or twenty-one-year-old visualized on that day. If you wish, you can skip this particular event, but for me, looking back, it was an important moment as I think this defining moment moulded me into what I am today. This event impacted me very strongly, and I came out stronger because of it.

Eventually, this burly man came in with some metal instruments and a plastic apron tied to his waist. He had a mask covering his face. None of us had any protective clothing to hide behind. Sometimes the masks that we wear hide our emotions, such as disgust, pain, or laughter.

Anyways, let me take you back to the burly man and the task at hand. The burly man adjusted himself at the side of the corpse he was going to work on. The corpse was a male adult of wheatish complexion, and I can see it clearly in my mind's eye as though it happened to me just yesterday.

Polishing his instruments, the burly man first made a semicircle incision on the patient's scalp from one ear to another. Then he proceeded to pull the skin of the corpse's scalp away. With precision, he pulled the skin downwards towards the face, up to the eyeballs, and just near the eyebrow line, he stopped. Similarly, he pulled the scalp's skin towards the nape of the neck.

As this was going on, there was pin-drop silence. We had no modern gadgets to film it, such as today's kids getting on with their mobiles and blasting it everywhere in a matter of seconds. Anyways, ethically as health-care providers, we do understand the confidentiality quotient of the nature of our job. It would be a breach of privacy and confidentiality for any one of us even today to post any such photos or videos on social media.

Once the skin was pulled away, either side of the skull was seen. It was dull creamy white. He then took his chisel and hammer, and he started neatly hammering away into the skull in the same semicircular fashion from ear to ear as we shocked onlookers watched on. He then managed to pry the skull open, and he scooped out the brain. He then kept the brain on a steel plate or tray. This steel plate or tray was kept nearby to receive the different internal organs required for the inspection. He left the whole skull open like an open coconut and proceeded towards the body. We just could not believe what was happening in front of our very eyes.

By then we discovered that some of us did not actually have the stomach for this, and they left as they were getting sick. I somehow was unable to leave, held there by some unidentified emotion. The burly man then made an incision from the hollow groove in the neck, below the Adam's apple, till just about somewhere below the navel. He then proceeded to open the chest and abdomen. The chest was a challenge, and he pried it open with some pliers. He took out some of the vital internal abdominal organs and started explaining to us. He then started doing chop-chop on all the organs that he had displayed on the steel tray. After completing his task, he sutured it all back with a huge needle and thread. He was like a cobbler who was at work. He did a very clumsy, untidy job of it, and irregularities were plenty. The finished job was ghastly looking. Finally, he went to the skull, closed it shut, pulled back the skin, and sewed it too.

On that day I learnt two things; one is that human relationships are the most important element in life, your present moments to live in. Death is an inevitable occurrence for each one of us, and we have to be prepared for it; live life one day at a time. The second thing I learnt is that some of us are bestowed with a strong stomach and fearless hearts to brave things or circumstances that not all can brave. It is a blessing as we are in need of those with this quality. Despite all that we see, touch, or smell daily, a good night's sleep is still ours for the taking. I count it as a blessing that up till now I do not have nightmares to disturb me.

Finally, I graduated not at the top of my class, not even close to it, yet armed with a degree that gave me the licence to practise as a registered nurse.

The Horror of Burns

We must embrace pain and burn
it as fuel for our journey.

Kenji Miyazawa

For me, the most difficult assignment was paediatrics, but somehow I managed to complete it, knowing fully well that it was not my passion. Sick little babies who were helpless disturbed me, and so I decided not to follow that line of practice later on. The one moment that probably made up my mind and heart was the following event.

As a student nurse, I had the misfortune to see the horror of burns in a tragic way. He was a toddler with about ninety per cent burns. For burns, we have a method where we calculate the surface of body area burnt according to percentage. We follow the rule of nines. For example, each lower limb (the anterior lower limb and posterior lower limb) is 9 per cent, which makes the leg 18 per cent; the anterior torso and posterior torso is 18 per cent; and so on and so forth.

There was no skin left on his little body, and he looked horribly pale in colour. I shall retell the story that I heard from the mother of this little baby. It seems they lived in a shanty in the famous Dharavi slums of Mumbai, which *Slumdog Millionaire* made so famous. They lived in one of the one-room slum houses all lined up one after the other. The single room was all they had, and it doubled up as a bedroom, kitchen, as well as a living room. The toilet privileges were always located outside the house while one could manage to bathe inside the house. It was noontime, and the mother was at home, just completing her many household chores for the day.

A pot of rice was cooking over the fire on a portable kerosene stove as they could not afford the luxury of a proper gas cooker. This kerosene stove was placed atop the table or a kitchen platform (or *kadapa*, a black stone platform, as it is known). The mother left the toddler in the miniscule room and went outside to take a quick pee. Those two minutes changed her entire life. The toddler was alone, probably bored. Attracted by the bright orange of the flame, he reached out to the stove and started to shake it. The pot of boiling rice toppled over the frail body. Hearing the screeches of her baby, the mother ran into the room to see what had befallen him.

Not knowing any better, the mother reached out to the baby and ripped off the clothes of the baby and, in doing so, also took the skin along with it. We worked tirelessly with that little baby, swathing his petite body with dressings, and resuscitating him with the much-needed intravenous fluids. But we lost the battle as the area of his burnt skin was too much for him to survive. I was heartbroken and decided that day that paediatrics was not for me. This was my first experience of a mother's anguish and a child's pain.

Part III

Walk along with Me

Do not go, where the path may lead, go instead
where there is no path and leave a trail.

Ralph Waldo Emerson

Walk with me through the hustle and bustle of
an everyday occurrence in a hospital. This
is our battlefield, where we save lives and prevent
harm as much as possible. If you were to walk inside
a hospital on any given day, this is the scene which
may greet you. During the day, through the hospital
corridors, you would find starched white uniforms
or coats, staff scurrying around with urgency, and
anxious patients and their families with looks of fear
and uncertainty etched on their faces. Every look that
we receive has questions, has hope written all over. I
have learnt, no matter how hopeless the medical case
seems to us clinically, we have to acknowledge the
power of the unseen, the power of the unpredictable.

The first point of contact for a patient is usually
the ED or ER, which is a short-name form for
emergency department or *emergency room*. The
emergency department is filled with conflicting and
contradicting emotions, screams of pain and anguish
from the patients and their relatives, as well as the

high-end drama from the physicians, nurses, and other health-care providers as they provide very urgent health care. There were ambulance sirens screeching, emergency bells being rung to alert you that a critical patient is being brought in for your care, and absolutely catastrophic casualties being brought on stretchers while police reports are being filed and medicolegal issues follow. Most of the road traffic accidents, homicide cases, suicides, and any other industrial or trauma accident victims find themselves inside the ED. The ever-present smell of pungent phenyl, pus, blood, and all sorts of body secretions and excretions were our everyday sight and smell that we took in our stride.

Life is hectic, fast-paced, and dynamic in the emergency department. The staff in the emergency department very rarely have the luxury of sitting down for meals; for them, they have only the provision of hurried meals. Yet it is one of the most rewarding departments in terms of satisfaction that your actions may have a direct impact on a person's life. Here is where you make a difference.

I have been fortunate to have a long stint in the emergency department, and I say *fortunate* with grace as this experience has humbled me and awakened me. I have been posted in other areas and units, but the longest duration has been in the ED, which I have come to appreciate over the years; it has grown on me. In the ED, there is no routine, and in no way can you describe it as monotonous. One gets addicted to the adrenaline rush, and you could spend years toiling away in the ED. The humble banana, for a very long time, had been my most precious companion.

It provided me with instant energy, and it was sterile as you did not need to wash a banana. And it could be eaten in a matter of a few minutes—very often in the women's toilet as toilet breaks were the only breaks we were permitted when we were very busy.

The patient volume that comes through the ED doors on any given day could range from an average of 200 to 400 patients. This is a twenty-four-hour statistics. To add to this, hospitals are also the place to accept all dead bodies for certification. So also for me, dead patients were brought in on a daily basis. Yet we could not keep these bodies as space was an issue, and so we transferred these bodies to the region's police mortuary. The reason I am mentioning this is to give you an idea that we accept death as an inevitable part of our lives.

On any given day, we definitely had to deal with at least two patients who may be brought in dead, or they were brought in a critical condition or had suffered a cardiac arrest. We deal with emergencies and near-death experiences all the time and take it as part of our daily occurrences. Initially, these death experiences were raw and very emotional, then over time, repetition makes it a little easier, but it is never mundane because this is someone passing away from this life. We learnt to camouflage our emotions and put up a brave front, but we do have our fears. Especially when we know that the patient's death is inevitable, the dread creeps in. Sometimes if the patient's death hits me hard and I feel the tears threatening to flow, I would make a last-minute dash to the women's toilet, which was always my sanctuary for various reasons.

Let's move away from the ED. I am shifting the gear towards our work schedules to give you an idea of our time schedules. Our shifts could be either eight-, ten-, or twelve-hour shifts. The eight-hour shifts usually run from around 07.00–15.00, 15.00–23.00, or 23.00–07.00. You might rotate day–evening shifts, evening–night shifts, or night–day shifts. You might work straight evenings or straight nights. Evening shifts, stretch from 15.00 till 23.00 and exhaust you in the bargain. On this shift, you cannot sit down to a decent lunch or dinner. Night shifts known as the graveyard shifts are another story altogether; eerie silence prevails in the hospital unless you are stationed in the emergency department as it never really witnesses peace. In all other areas in the hospital, lights get turned off during the night, and dimmers are switched on, but the emergency department is one such department that never sleeps.

For most physicians and nurses, acquiring horrendous eating habits is a way of life. This is the downside of this profession, yet all this makes you very flexible and ready to adapt to whatever comes your way. All nurses need to have a pair of sturdy legs to carry their weight around as sitting is hardly a privilege for the job at hand.

The more-sophisticated hospitals have an overhead paging system which could alert hospital personnel any time they are needed. Additionally, the hospital may have code announcements going on, for which we have to be alert at all times. Let me tell you some of the different code systems that we normally have in hospitals. The codes when announced always specify the location within the hospital.

The first one and the most important is the code blue/crash code, which if alerted means that one of our patients has had a cardiac arrest and has collapsed. This could occur anywhere in the hospital, and a team gets activated to assist with the resuscitation. A crash trolley, a defibrillator, and emergency medications are brought along for the resuscitation. Then we may have a code to manage security issues or violent patients—code black. It is also mandatory to have a code given for a fire alert, which could be called code orange. Now these various codes are announced on the overhead system in this manner so that patients are not alarmed and everything is managed very smoothly—no need for panic.

Heartbreaking is the oncology unit, which deals with cancer patients and very often the terminally ill. Cancer does not select but makes contact with all ages and all social classes—the rich, the poor, and the middle class. This is another area of the hospital which is gut-wrenching and needs immense strength to hold on to your corner of peace and tranquillity.

Happy and joyful is the obstetric unit of hospitals as bundles of joy are brought into this world at regular intervals. The miracle unfolding before you time and time again is an absolute joy to see. Occasionally, we do have sad endings in this area, but generally obstetrics has evolved, and successful endings are the norm.

The psychiatric units or wards can altogether depress the health-care provider in the long run as you come into contact with individuals who are physically fit individuals but whose minds are not tuned in. It is an extremely sensitive unit, and for those patients and their near and dear ones, you ought to have the utmost compassion. There is also the hint of potential danger as patients can harm themselves as well as the others surrounding them. Security is a priority in this unit, and nurses are well trained and skilled to provide expert care—or rather, that is the way it should be.

The intensive care unit is another high-risk area. In short, it is known as the ICU, and I really believe it is called that as it needs constant patient observation from us at all times. Each hospital will identify the different types of specialized ICUs it needs to cater to their patient population. So today we may have a general ICU, a coronary care/cardiac unit, or an infectious ICU. There is usually a central monitor, which allows a nurse to observe the individual cardiac monitors from a central vintage point. Most of our ICU patients are critical, who may linger over a thin line between life and death. Nurses who are assigned in these units have to be commended as they are a group of highly skilled, competent, and trained professionals. Some of these patients may be comatose or be hooked up to a ventilator. As the patient is in a coma, most often it is the family that needs our attention; it is them who have questions, are anxious, and need our reassurance. It is a difficult situation to be in for the family, and we try our level best to be there for them. Equally difficult it is for the nurses as they deal with high-risk, intense stress 24/7.

Another area I must mention is the OT, which in short is *operation theatre*. This is one area which is completely restricted to the patient's family and relatives because of the sterile nature of the OT environment. In the OT, most of our patient–nurse interactions are limited to after the patient is brought into the OT and induced under anaesthesia. The OT team is very focused with the task in hand, and very few distractions interrupt the team.

Added to this mixture of departments are all the auxiliary units, and the list is exhausting. We coordinate and interact like one big team to deliver holistic and cohesive health care to our patients and their families.

Health care has evolved both in infrastructure as well as in practice. What used to be hospitals with whitewashed walls have now been transformed into five-star-hotel-type health-care organizations with all the amenities available during your convalescence. Nowadays, when you step into a hospital, it feels like you are stepping into a five-star hotel to have a five-course meal and be swept into culinary heaven rather than have your liver biopsy procedure done. The lobby of a sophisticated, modern hospital may have contemporary coffee houses, a trendy grocery or supermarket of sorts, and at times, even a beauty salon for all your maintenance needs.

A hospital is an amalgamation of skills, complex situations, and high-risk circumstances. And Nurses are the foundation and building blocks of any hospital.

What's a Typical Workday in A Nurse's Life?

Don't go through life, grow through life.

Eric Butterworth

As we come on duty, irrespective of the shift, we do so with a whisper of a prayer in our hearts. We then proceed to take a report from the outgoing nursing shift. Following the shift-change report, we then do a walk around and do a quick once-over look at our patients to check that all patients are present, that none have gone missing, and that all are alive and kicking, especially if you are assigned in an emergency room or ICU as this would be absolutely necessary. This shift-change report is mandatory and should not be missed by any member of the staff; doing so will cost you a very strict reprimand from the captain of the ship. Information is often passed on by the outgoing nurse in what is called a shift-over report. It is extremely important that the outgoing nurse pass on accurate information. The rest of the day will depend on the accuracy of that report, which will be our creed for the day. So what information the nurse puts into the report is important, and the outgoing nurse will be legally accountable for it.

Once the outgoing shift leaves the unit and the small chit-chat is over, we then proceed to once again do a more detailed assessment of our assigned patients. We prioritize patient care depending on immediate needs of our patients. During a working day, all these and more are done between numerous interruptions from patients, relatives, patients' escorts, and phone calls from various areas, such as laboratory results, physicians wishing to find out information, and different departments where the patient needs to be sent.

Who needs what and how quickly—it's all about knowing what needs are more important than others, what lab tests or procedures have been done, or what's waiting to be done. Medication charts are checked to verify existing orders and to ensure that there are no new orders to follow up. We then either document it in the medical health records or provide treatments, such as dressing changes. Depending on which unit we are stationed in, we deal with basic to specialized patient care. Trachea care (which involves inducing a hole in the windpipe to enable the patient to breathe) may require our attention, and so does intravenous care, such as changing intravenous lines or infusion bottles, transporting patients, and using complicated, heavy haemodynamic and ventilator (breathing) equipment. Additionally, we deal with tubes for all jobs, such as suction or infusion tubes. Add to this, we also deal with enemas, bedpans, and kidney trays or K trays for all secretions and excretions. Initially in my career, we had to clean the bedpans and K trays in a bedpan washer, but technology has made our lives easier with disposables at our disposal. In a day's work, we also score our patients against specific predetermined criteria and put in strategies to prevent patient falls and injuries.

We work hard long hours, and we are challenged in every imaginable way. We get patients out of bed when they do not have the physical strength to do so themselves. We delegate some tasks (like bathing, feeding, etc.) to the assistive personnel, like nursing assistants or a practical nurse, if we don't have time to do those tasks ourselves. For twenty-four-hour medical health-record reviews, you document every little thing that you do for your patient either on paper or on a computerized medical health record. It was assumed "not done" if you did not document it. That is the golden rule of documentation.

The busiest times of our shifts are in the morning, when most of the departments are operational and all our work needs to get completed. The night shifts are quieter but pose a challenge to some of us. Our normal body clocks go for a toss, and we have to drink cups of coffee or tea to keep awake. For those nurses who have families and chores to complete during the day, night duties are usually painful. When we are on duty, dozing off is definitely not permitted. Imagine sleepy nurses trying to deal with critical patients. That would be asking for trouble.

We were overwhelmed when we could not cope with the very busy days. We often got road traffic accidents, cardiac patients, and burn patients all coming in together. All these patients needed our expert skill mix, long resuscitation periods, fortitude, and patience. There have been times when I have been exhausted and bone-tired—if you know what that means. And after reaching home at twelve midnight after an afternoon shift, because you are so keyed up with all that adrenaline pumping or coursing through your veins, you are unable to sleep. You drift off to sleep only by about 1 a.m. or 1.30 a.m. if you are lucky enough.

During my very first posting, I was particularly tired one day after a morning shift and reached home around four in the evening. I knew the next day I was off, so after a meal by five in the evening, I decided to catch up on some much-needed sleep. I drew the curtains and tried to make the room as dark as possible to cheat my brain into believing it was already night-time. I put on the air con and drifted off to sleep.

I finally woke up a little disoriented and noted the time to be five thirty but was not sure that this five thirty was morning or evening; you know, there are times you get a bit groggy and confused as soon as you get up. I proceeded to freshen up and find out the actual time. I was shocked to note that I had actually slept a straight twenty-four hours with exhaustion and could not even remember if I had taken any toilet breaks in this twenty-four-hour slumber. I have never repeated this pattern again and was very mindful to set myself alarm clocks in the future.

In our world, there is no room for slack as errors and consequential patient harm are irreversible. The cost is too high in terms of human life. All our strategies and actions are focused on the prevention of patient harm and errors. The creed we follow is *primum nil nocere*, a Latin phrase which means 'no harm', and the care we provide is focused on 'no patient harm'.

After telling you about our typical day, I am sure one of the questions that comes to your mind is about the embarrassment you feel when you may have to undress so that we can do our duty. I can assure you that we do not focus on that aspect. We do not mention it or make jokes about it or laugh over it.

Even when you are undressed and are being examined by us, we respect you. Though it seems that we are looking at you, we are not really looking at your body form or shape. We have to see or observe you from up close to make our clinical decisions or conclusions.

Talking about embarrassment, I must tell you an incident where I was embarrassed or rather shy.

The hospital where I started out as an RN had ward boys only during the day shift and had none for the evening. It meant that all patients' scheduled surgeries were confirmed the previous day and all patients on this scheduled list were prepped by the ward boy—at least, the shaving. I was on the afternoon shift, and a young adult male patient was brought in for an emergency appendectomy. That meant I was required to prep this patient and get him ready for surgery. Being twenty-two years of age and with a young male patient, I was reluctant to do so. I was not mature enough to look the patient in the eyes while I had to shave, clean, and prepare him for surgery. I was close to tears as I could not confide my reluctance to the surgeon, who would definitely chide me. I was at my wit's end and really left with no option but to stride into the patient's room. I am forever obliged to my knight, who rescued me from this particular predicament. He was the resident physician who, after seeing my distress, actually offered to prep the patient. I have never ever seen another physician—at least in my term as a nurse—who would offer to do such a menial job as shaving. So do understand that it is not you at times who are shy or frightened; with the nature of our job, so are we. In time, I learnt that I had to grow out of it if I had to do all aspects of my job and without shirking my responsibilities.

For soap and water enemas, earlier on through the years, we actually had to manually mix a solution of soap and warm water to administer enemas. Glass syringes that needed to be resterilized were used as we did not have access to disposables or single-use syringes, which would have been a luxury in our days if we ever got our hands on them.

Even latex gloves were introduced only in the early nineties; till then, for surgical procedures, we used sterile surgical glove packs, which came individually packed according to the size number. Latex gloves came much later and were in three standard sizes— that would be small, medium, and large—and you somehow managed to fit in. Nowadays, of course there are many different options, with latex-free gloves for those of us who are sensitive or allergic to latex gloves.

Here are some of the questions that plague us almost constantly on a daily basis: Did I forget to tell the incoming nurse something important about my patient? Did I sign off a medication I administered? Did I leave a patient in the toilet and forget to tell anyone?

But I must say that during the times I was with patients, I found solace; it wasn't all about the race against time or the very important documentation. We value and respect our patients. They are people, not just diagnoses; They are people with an identity of their own. We try to see the person behind the patient, who could be obscured by wires, medical tape, and breathing tubes. Sometimes due to the nature of our work, we may seem much focused on the mechanical skills, but time and again, we remind ourselves that this is a life we are treating. Relatives and patients' families wish to care for their loved ones themselves, yet with great difficulty and reluctance, they leave us to take care of the patients, bestowing a huge responsibility on our shoulders, which we try to not let down.

I have realized over the years that at times it may not even occur to us what impact we have on our patients and their families. On numerous times, we may have smiled or reassured our patients, and that smile might have brought warmth to someone's troubled heart. I do hope that there have not been many times that we have snapped or been rude to our patients and their families. These random acts may not matter to us when we actually do something for our patients or for their families, but I can tell you that these acts are forever imprinted in the minds and hearts of our patients and their families. They may not remember or even be aware of how skilfully we inserted the intravenous infusion but will remember the warm moments when we shared and cared for them. It may be a small act of bringing a warm cup of coffee, a warm touch, or maybe even our one-second eye contact that gives them strength, but these small moments are what we have to put above all into our practice. This is not taught in textbooks but is within us, inherent, helps, heals, and touches. In addition to all our medical expertise, this brings a human element to the cold, sterile world of a hospital.

My patients helped me open my eyes to the diversity of human experience—the different emotions, situations, and circumstances. We make an unbearable situation more pleasant for someone by providing support to those in need and advocating for our patients. Nurses will hold your hand figuratively or literally and remind you that you are not alone and that your life is valued even if sometimes it cannot be saved.

For a Few Laughs

I have seen what a laugh can do. It can
transform almost unbearable tears into
something bearable, even hopeful.

Bob Hope

We also do get hilarious and outrageous
incidents at times to lighten the mood.
There was this one time when I was on a night shift.
Around 4 a.m., the cops strolled in with a man who
was fairly short in height. The man was handcuffed.
Now it was a light night shift, and we were all in a
very relaxed mood.

It looked like the man was actually arrested by the
cops. The organization where I worked also had to
inspect and examine cases needed for legal aspects.
Anyways getting back to the story, we proceeded to
find out what was actually the problem. We found
out that it was a case of bestiality which is a sexual act
between man and animal, and this man was caught
in the act with a sheep. So we waited patiently for the
emergency medical record to come by us so that the
doctor could document his findings.

When the emergency medical record came, the
doctor called me to his side and pointed out that the

registration clerk had written 'screwed a cow' as the chief complaint. So I walked over to the registration desk, pretty amused by then, and explained to the registration clerk that the animal was a sheep, and I imitated a sheep to make a point. 'Baeh! Baeh!' I then came back to the examination room and once again waited for the emergency medical record.

After a few minutes, we heard the doctor rather loudly calling all of us to come to his side. To our amusement, the emergency medical record had been documented now to state 'screwed a ship'. And once again, I proceeded to the registration clerk to make my point until it was rightly changed, but that was the mood of that night, light and full of laughter.

The Communication Book

On a lighter note, something to bring a smile, let me talk about the communication book, which is a book kept in the unit so that we could read it for any important notes. As we work on different shifts and may not meet each other, this was one way to communicate with each other in the times when WhatsApp, Twitter, and Facebook were not around. Whatever had to be communicated to the team was written down and dated. And the team acknowledged by signing that each one of us had read the communication.

The following was written in the communication book, which definitely brought on a giggle or two from the team who were made to read it.

'Please keep your pantry clean.' Where is the humour in that, you may ask? Well, the charge nurse, while documenting, had forgotten the *r* in *pantry*.

Another one was the communication note related to patient referrals which stated, 'Refer to Public Health Clinic.' Well, the very same charge nurse had not learnt a lesson in typo mistakes and once again made a blunder by omitting the *l* in *public*.

On a lighter note, I also recollect that we had a very vocal charge nurse. This charge nurse used to joke around with all the nurses who were blessed with ample headlights and tail lights—if you know what I mean. They became the brunt of her jokes, and the nurses were called MBBS (member of so and so), depending on whether the nurse had ample head- or tail lights. I am sure most of us took it in our stride as these were some of our avenues to vent out our stress, and I can say that I was the brunt of a lot of jokes with my chubby frame. At least, we can safely say that we tend not to get too sensitive in our profession, and should one be sensitive, we then did not pursue any personal jokes with that person. Everything was done in good jest with no intention to malign anyone.

On Call, While Travelling Too

To travel is to take a journey into yourself.

Danny Kaye

For most of us, journeys and holidays are fun and a time to relax. Over here, I wish to remind you that as medical or paramedical staff, it seems like we are on call all the time. Imagine you are flying on a commercial flight, and one of the passengers becomes sick and collapses, then the overhead aircraft announcement requests for a physician or a nurse. Now the nurse or physician in question needs to stand up and identify themselves to assist, but what if they themselves are inebriated and cannot be of much help?

As health-care providers, I think we have a duty towards the community and should be responsible. With the call of duty, at times we were required to accompany patients on flights as medical escort. I once had to escort a patient with lung cancer whose left lung had collapsed. As a preparation for this journey, we had to ensure that I had access to oxygen throughout the flight. I travelled alone with the patient, who was able to sit through the flight. I had to make sure that oxygen was administered and that he was comfortable and pain-free as much as possible. It was a considerable short flight of about three hours, yet in those three hours, I was scared and kept imagining horrific scenes involving my patient. For the whole flight, my fingers were fixated on his pulse point, and I prayed that during ascent and descent of the flight, his lungs could endure the difference in pressure. It was only once we arrived at our destination that I heaved a sigh of relief. It was a huge burden to ensure that I could responsibly escort him on his journey home.

It's one thing to be on duty as a medical escort on a flight and another thing altogether to be travelling on a holiday and sometimes be called due to the fact that some fellow passengers could not handle their alcoholic drinks and got sick on the flight. There could be other times too when passengers genuinely need your medical expertise, but I do hope those times are by far very few as on flights we will not have the environment or the resources required to provide emergency care.

Rude and Obnoxious Behaviour Is Not Becoming of a Nurse

Charm, I think, is education, really, no?
I was educated to be nice to everybody.
If you want to be rude and mean,
I'm sure your life isn't that nice.

Mario Testino

There was a time that I was on a night shift. I was stationed in a female medical ward. It was a light night, with all our patients tucked in. We did not receive any new admissions and had no urgent patient call bells to attend to. It was a peaceful night. I was actually just starting out as a registered nurse still in my first year of practice, a new gal amongst all the veterans.

One of our inpatients was a young lady in her early thirties who was suffering from leukaemia, and she was quite sick. Having nothing much to do, I was taking an inspection walk around the ward. When I peeped into her room, though it was late, she was not yet asleep. So I entered the room to ask why she was not sleeping. I could also provide some painkillers or sleeping pills as that is mostly the case with terminally ill patients, so I ventured inside to offer just that. She was visibly upset, and she told me, 'I wish my husband were here. At least he would press my legs.' As it was a female ward, male escorts were restricted and were not permitted overnight stay.

Feeling immensely sad for her as we could not permit her husband to escort her, I started pressing her legs. Touch can do wonders; a little caring was all she needed that night. While doing that, I started having a soft conversation with her. When she drifted off to sleep, I left her, and I returned to the nursing station. Now at the nursing station, the nurses were just gossiping, but on seeing me return back, the senior nurses wanted to know what took me so long. I did relate to them what had happened. Expecting a positive feedback, I was taken aback when one of the senior nurses became angry with me.

Now you have to hear her out and the reason for her anger. The senior veteran nurses were angry that I actually went to press this patient's legs and bring comfort to her tired, aching body. They actually told me not to go around doing this and make our patients accustomed to this as they will get habituated and ask the same from the remaining nurses.

It was at that time that I whispered a prayer that even if I advance in years in the nursing field, it will not make me so immune that I will not care any more and I become mechanical in the job. Though I must say, for every uncaring practising nurse, there are loads of caring, compassionate nurses whose aim is to spread warmth around, along with the nursing skill and competence that we provide.

For Better or for Worse

Maybe this one moment, with this
one person, is the very reason we're
here on this Earth at this time.

Anonymous

It was a prayer from my heart that I sent often enough during the time that I cared for him. My heart was heavy as I knew the inevitable would descend on us. I implored and begged from the core of my heart that I may not be present when his end came as I was not sure that I would be strong enough to endure his passing away in front of me. To tell you about the outcome of the end, I must start at the beginning of their story.

They were a couple in their early forties; they were married pretty late. He was from an affluent family, and she was from a family that was way below their social status. His family did not take it lightly that he had married beneath their social stature. So they decided to live separately from his family and moved out of the family home. As fate or destiny would have it, within the first year of their marriage, he was diagnosed with cancer of the tongue. After a few referrals, they met with an oncologist, who broke the bad news to them.

His consulting oncologist offered surgery coupled with different treatment modalities. During the late eighties, undergoing surgery was not without its pitfalls, and cancer was a dreaded disease. HIV was not yet well known. Even people in a cosmopolitan city were not better informed and did not have access to accurate information. In those days, the Uncle Google technology was uncommon. Nowadays, even a layman will reach out to technology to figure out the symptoms of his ailment to assist him in searching for information. Tongues wagged, and rumours and gossip influenced one and all about horrific cancer tragedies. So this newly married couple also had to hear a lot related to the impending surgery that was advised for his newly diagnosed cancer, and this impacted them negatively.

He declined surgery and opted for alternate treatment modality, such as radiation and chemotherapy. The treatment provided did not arrest the growth of the tumour, and soon there were metastases, the spread of the cancer in other areas of the body. In no time, he was deemed terminal. Though the couple was admitted in a semi-private room, which permitted two patients to cohabit together, we could not put any other patient in his room because of the stench.

When I met him, honestly I must tell you that none of the floor nurses wanted to be assigned to take care of him. Initially, out of no other choice, he was assigned in my care. I was a fresh graduate and not very confident at that time of my nursing skills.

So with apprehension, I strode into their lives. He looked like a Frankenstein monster with half his face missing. The right side of his face had burst open, showing remnants of half a cheek, and the right eye was swollen and closed. The right ear was not visible; it seemed to have been eaten away. Rotting, putrid flesh with maggots squirming in the wound was visible. The movements of the maggots continuously disturbed him. My initial apprehension diminished when I got to know the couple.

From a healthy six-footer, he had drastically transformed into a skeletal frame with skin and bones. He was given liquids, which he swallowed with great difficulty. They refused feeding tubes to be inserted. When he desired to taste a particular food, we had to put small amounts into his mouth, which he would spit after chewing it in his mouth. Over a period of time, I formed a relationship with them, a bond which I cherished, as I witnessed a love which transcended all times.

Having got immune to the stench, I became their only pastime. His wife and I had cups of tea and pored over their married photos and memories. In his photographs, he seemed to be a handsome bearded six-footer with broad shoulders and fair complexion. What touched me to this day about their story was the devotion of the wife. She had met him over a casual acquaintance, got married, and stayed true to the sanctity of marriage. She painstakingly took maggots out of his wound with me, cleansed him, dried him, and practically stayed in that room 24/7. She never left his side to take a break from it all. I never had to call another nurse because the wife was always there. I salute his wife, and though her face is very sketchy to me over the period of many years, the memory of those days still reassures me of the warmth of human love.

Ah! Yes, my prayers were answered. That morning as I came on duty, I got to know he had just passed away. I was not present when he breathed his last, yet I was bestowed the privilege to dress him up for his last journey as I bid adieu to a man of great stature and his wife of even greater stature.

I thank God or divine grace or whatever name you refer to for giving me the opportunity to experience this great love that transcends everything. This was my first death experience where I had connected with both the patient and his family, and it stuck in my heart and mind forever. I was not promised that my chosen career path would be easy, but out of all this pain comes growth and strength to endure.

Sweat of Thy Brow

It's when we start working together that the real healing takes place . . . It's when we start spilling our sweat and not our blood.

David Hume

The hot summer months brought in scores of heat-exhaustion patients, mostly fourth-class workers who had to brave the weather in order to get their job done. They toiled in the sun, carrying heavy loads, and sometimes put in twelve hours of hard labour. These patients came in or were brought in parched and drenched in sweat. You could very literally squeeze sweat from their clothes.

I remember days when busloads of patients presented themselves in the ED on particularly hot days. There just weren't enough beds to accommodate all the patients, and we had to seat them on plastic chairs lined up against the wall. We had to improvise in order to provide the health care which was necessary for them. Some of them came in with severe cramps, with their fingers, hands, and feet in knots from lack of vital electrolytes.

We would then start intravenous drips while they sat, and we administered cool drinks to quench their thirst. Most of them would recover sufficiently by then; the few who would not recover needed blood workouts to ensure their blood electrolyte levels were within normal range. We did also get the occasional heatstroke patient who would be drifting into an unconscious state. This happens when the patient does not seek medical assistance during the heat-exhaustion state. Once a patient with heatstroke is brought to the hospital, we get into action. The temperature was always taken rectally as the patient was incapable of holding an oral thermometer in place. The thermometer would not register the temperature on it as the patient's temperature was higher than the degree noted on the thermometer.

This patient needed specialized care and was always admitted to the ICU. You could lose these patients due to the fact that they did not seek medical aid early enough or the unfortunate fact that medical aid was just not accessible to them. And by the time medical aid is administered, it is at times too late to salvage them.

Pink or Blue Has Another Hue, Which Is Grey

Where there is love, there is life.

Mahatma Gandhi

As I came on my shift duty, I was assigned to a woman in active labour in her fourth pregnancy—a multipara, as we in our medical lingo would have referred to her. She was highly distressed but not because of the physical nature of the labour. That she was used to, having delivered babies before, and I was sure even this delivery would be quick. She was in aguish as she was given an ultimatum. Her husband and his family demanded a baby boy from her after she had blessed them with three girls. The in-laws as well as her husband did not see the daughters as a blessing. This time around, her fourth pregnancy, an ultimatum was given to her. If the baby to be born would be a girl, then the in-laws and husband insisted that she would be out of the marriage. A new bride would be arranged in order to give the family the male heir they so desired.

So when I came on my shift in the afternoon at around 3 p.m., this mother was already in labour. At that time, the hospital that I worked in had an admission rule for deliveries. If the patient had been admitted into a general ward (which had cubicle beds separated by a curtain), then the patient would have to be delivered by the nurses. And if the pregnant lady was admitted in a private room admission or a semi-private room, then a physician would have to be in attendance to deliver the baby. This information was always conveyed to all expectant mothers as well as the family so that an informed decision could be taken.

This particular mother was admitted into the general ward, and it was my responsibility to deliver her baby. As soon as I came in and all throughout her labour, the woman kept pleading and imploring with me to give her a baby boy. This mother was in the throes of physical pain and mental distress. It was the only time that I ever bothered or was even worried about the sex of the child I was about to deliver. You see, we witness so many abnormal babies being born that we never take for granted that a healthy baby will be born. We nurses pray for a normal delivery with a healthy baby rather than any particular sex for the baby. Yet this time, I was as anxious as the mother waiting for the delivery. I felt her helplessness and despair. I thought about her three daughters and their fate. So as she was in the throes of labour, I fervently prayed for her wish to come true so that her fate would not be sealed on that day. I prayed for the peace of her family and her little girls.

So what do you think was the end of that story? I cannot keep you in any more suspense as I was on that day. She had a healthy baby boy and was so relieved with the exhaustion of the wait.

I went out of the labour suite to tell the father the news of the delivery. Normally, I would not be the one doing the job of declaring the news of the delivery, but this time around, I so wished to do it. After hearing that his wife had delivered a baby boy, the father immediately upgraded his wife to a private-room status from a general-admission status. The husband further insisted that we call in a physician for post-delivery consultation, and it was the physician who proceeded to do the rest of the post-delivery care.

We do not allow our personal prejudice or opinions to come in the way of the care that we provide. But so much for the today's modern world, with great infrastructure and remarkable technology, the world still insists on baby boys and puts the onus of the baby's sex on the mother. Yet the male gender does not comprehend that it is the father that determines the sex of the foetus to be born.

The Mother, the Child, and the Emergency Call

All that I am, or hope to be, I
owe to my Angel Mother.

Abraham Lincoln

It was late in the afternoon, and I was having a quiet moment by myself. It was my day off from a hectic shift schedule. Lingering over my cup of coffee, I had just settled down to a good read when I got a long-distance emergency call from my mother's neighbour to say that my mother was sick. I attempted to speak to my mother, and I realized that she was out of breath. I could not understand what she was saying. I realized that she was extremely breathless, and I requested my mother's neighbour to rush my mother to the nearby hospital. When my mum reached the emergency department, she was having severe breathing difficulty, and she had an oxygen saturation of only 53 per cent. To sustain life, humans need above 90 per cent oxygen saturation. The physician had a telephone discussion with me and obtained my permission. My mum was intubated and put on a ventilator to help her breathe.

In a matter of a few hours, I was at my mother's bedside. When I saw my mother, that moment was priceless for me. In that one moment, she became my baby and I her mother. She was conscious, and amidst the ventilator tube, she looked at me with imploring eyes. A picture could speak a thousand words, they say, and this one definitely did. She wished to have the tubes removed. She could not speak due to the tube in her mouth, a torture that is so great. Her eyes swelled up with tears. I sat down, cooing to her and reassuring her that no matter what, I would be there for her. I promised her that if her condition improved, we would get the tubes removed the very next day. And that was how the ICU waiting room episodes started for the next few days.

Motherhood is Painful

Your children are not your children. They are the
sons and daughters of life's longing for itself.
They come through you but not from you.
And though they are with you, yet
they belong not to you.

Khalil Gibran

I met her in the waiting room allotted to the family
and relatives of the patients in the ICU. She
intrigued me as you do not see many female relatives
especially during the night; this is mostly occupied by
the male relatives of the patients. The waiting room
was very sparse and had the bare minimum furniture
just enough to keep your weary head down for the
night. Not that any one of us was going to get a
good night's sleep. There was an intercom/telephone
in the room, which was connected to the ICU. Every
time it rang, it brought shivers down our spines. With
all my nursing knowledge and experience, even I
would take a deep breath every time the phone rang;
what more for the lay person who had no idea or
inkling of the medical world.

Through the dark, still nights that I spent in the
ICU waiting room, I met this woman. Her faith was

immovable, and there was brilliance about her. Her strength showed through her eyes, and you could see she was the rock that you could lean on to. To most of us, she is known as a *mother*. To me, she was in pain, in agony, and I reached out to her. When she knew that I was a nurse, she gravitated towards me for any comfort that I could give her. Her daughter, aged twenty-seven years, was battling for her life. She had been married for less than a year. It seems that she had contracted simple fever and flu-like symptoms, for which she did visit a general physician, their family doctor.

Initially, the family doctor gave her some flu tablets and sent her away. When the fever did not subside and the daughter did not get any better, she was taken to a nursing home for investigating the cause of the fever. It was then that they found out that the daughter had the deadly form of malaria, which is falciparum malaria. She was hospitalized in the nursing home, and within a couple of days, her condition started deteriorating. She was then shifted to a hospital that was better equipped to manage her treatment, and that was how she landed in the very same hospital that my mother was admitted to.

When I met the mother, the daughter was critical and was transferred to the ICU, and the physicians decided to provide ventilator support for the daughter. Before giving consent to being hooked on a ventilator, all her daughter asked her mother was 'Will I be okay?' Other than nodding, the mother could not do much more. The daughter was attached to a ventilator.

The mother was distraught yet strong. She was in so much pain and grief, but she never cried, holding on to her pain and strength and living in hope. I could feel it in every moment that I spent with the mother. It was a brief encounter of maybe three days, but it touched that part of my soul which I do not normally permit while taking care of patients. Usually, the understanding is, if we as nurses get emotional with each and every patient and their relatives, it will be difficult for us to perform our duties to the best of our abilities. Though we empathize with the different patient situations, we try not to allow emotion to cloud our critical and clinical judgements. But here, I was not performing any nursing duty. I was not required to exhibit any nursing skills, so I let my guard down.

I continued to meet the mother as we both literally lived in that dingy waiting room day and night. While my mother recovered and was shifted away from the ICU, the other mother was still ever present in the waiting room, waiting for a ray of sunshine, waiting for a ray of hope. I guess that is why they call it waiting room—as you are caught waiting . . .

I was no longer required to stay overnight in the waiting room. I moved in with my mother in the room allotted to her. Yet I kept in touch with the mother and continued contact whenever I could. Every time I had to run errands for needed medications or medical supplies, I made it a point to stop by this waiting room to meet this grief-stricken mother. All this time, she was resilient and strong, a fortress that no one could shake. My mother was discharged from the hospital, and soon came the day that I had to leave. On my last day, before departure, I went for a last hug and a prayer on my lips to meet the mother who still sat in the waiting room, waiting.

I returned back to the faraway land and resumed my normal hospital duties, and though the grief-stricken mother did cross my mind, I was too engrossed and preoccupied with the job at hand to put in a long-distance call. It was about three weeks since I had met her.

It was my day off, and I was relaxing, but my heart was troubled. I could not shake off the discomfort that I was feeling. This mother somehow was on my mind that early morning on my day off. I couldn't put my heart to rest, so I finally called the mother to enquire how her daughter was doing.

I now know why my heart was troubled and restless. When I called, I was told that the daughter had breathed her last the very same morning that I was feeling restless. It sent gooseflesh over my body, and I vowed that next time around I will not be so engrossed in mundane everyday things because maybe someone somewhere needs you more than you need your solitude and space.

Talking about mothers and daughters brings me to another heart-warming story about mothers and what they endure.

Love Is the Thread That Connects All of Us

A baby is God's opinion that life should go on.

Carl Sandburg

Love is a connection, a stirring of the soul that keeps the body alive against all odds. They came into this world together on the same day. They were twin baby girls; both were fair, with beautiful creamy translucent skin, green eyes—adorable. But there ends the similarity as one was normal while the other was born with so many abnormalities. This little special, petite baby was most beautiful-looking with her huge green-grey eyes and creamy skin, yet she was a completely flaccid, limp baby with a huge hump on her back, having no feeding or sucking reflex. We had to feed her with a tube, known as a nasogastric tube, which was pushed gently into one of her nostrils and reached into her stomach. The mother would express her breast milk to be fed into her tube. Her stronger twin grew into an amazing little bundle of joy, and she was discharged along with her mother. The weak baby could not be discharged, and she was kept under our care in the hospital.

What is touching and the most amazing part of this story is the little girls' family. From the grandparents, parents, uncles, and aunts, there were daily visits from every single one of them for a whole year and a half as the little baby girl was hospitalized for a long time. During visits, the family hugged and caressed the little one, cuddled her like she was going to break, like a little porcelain doll.

They celebrated her life's first birthday by dressing her up in a beautiful pink dress and bringing all the nurses tokens of their appreciation. It was a special birthday party that really warmed my heart and brought tears to my soul. Things continued as usual for a long time.

One night we gave up on the little baby girl, and we informed the family that she may not make it through the night. The family was prepared for the inevitable. That night, all we did was administer oxygen and wipe the froth or perform suction on her as delicately as possible. We were informed that no active resuscitation was to be carried out on the little baby girl. I really did think that this was it, the end of this little baby girl. During that night, the family rallied around her, surrounded the cradle, prayed, sang, cuddled, and touched her as much as possible. We broke all visitor rules for them.

Yes, I did tell you at the start of this story that love conquers all. And despite the fact that there was no active medical intervention or resuscitation, the little bundle pulled through that night, and everyone was back to cooing over her during everyday visiting hours.

Miracles Are Everywhere;
You Just Have to Feel Them

There are two ways to live:
you can live as if nothing is a miracle,
you can live as if everything is a miracle.

Albert Einstein

Now that I have told you so much about pain, I will tell you a story that touched my heart in a very different way. I was involved in a project to measure out-of-hospital resuscitation statistics in collaboration with the region's ambulance systems. My daily work entailed documenting the number of patients who were brought in with an out-of-hospital cardiac arrest and who were resuscitated on the field or site. The project was focused on collecting data for the patients who survived. Most of the patients in this project had negative outcomes if they survived (it meant most of the time that they were ventilated), and eventually, after a couple of days, they succumbed to the cardiac arrest. Or were declared DOA or dead on arrival. Meaning they were brought into the hospital dead and that is why the terminology Dead On Arrival. A very small percentage of this group survived, but they were unable to completely recover and manage their activities of daily living independently. The following story is an amazing encounter with a patient from this study group.

One such patient was a male patient who felt some uneasiness in his chest and did go to see a free, stand-alone outpatient's clinic. In the clinic, as part of the diagnostics workout, they did take his ECG (an electrocardiogram which traces the electric activity of the heart and is diagnostic in nature). As they were taking the ECG, the patient suffered a massive cardiac arrest and a ventricular fibrillation, a cardiac arrhythmia which is fatal in clinical outcome. Active resuscitation was carried out, and his heart was given repetitive cardiac shocks. This patient was finally ventilated and shifted out to the hospital.

He was then admitted into the coronary care unit of the hospital in which I worked. Specialized care was administered—as is provided for all such patients. And then lo and behold, as if a miracle, after three days this patient was extubated or weaned off from the ventilator. He made a full recovery, with absolutely no residual negative changes. This is one of the rarest cases that I have witnessed in my nursing career. The patient in question is very appreciative of his near-death experience, and so are we who came into contact with him. In a place that sometimes we get to see so much misery, we were overjoyed to experience this amazing miracle unfold before our eyes.

Because this patient is so special, I still bump into him now and then at supermarkets or delis. I guess this is God's way of reminding me time after time that miracles do exist. And every time I meet him, I guess we are both wrapped up in this awe of life that he was blessed with.

The Truth Hurts but Must Be Told

There are two ways of exerting one's strength;
one is pushing down, the other is pulling up.

Booker T. Washington

An equally painful experience that I had to witness was that of a young lady in her twenties. She was about twenty-five years old. She was brought in one afternoon, with about 25 per cent burns over her body.

I have in my nursing career witnessed many burn injuries and really horrid events, but the element of shock in this story was that this was not a fresh-burn incident but three days old. So when she was brought in, I wanted to know why she subjected herself to this pain by staying away from a hospital. Actually, I was horrified that anyone could allow this to happen to them. And this is her story.

She was married to a man much older than her age. Her married life was not a happy life, but full of fights. With her husband's drunken behaviour, domestic violence was an everyday occurrence she had to endure. When matters came to a head and went above her tolerance level, she unfortunately attempted suicide by setting herself on fire. Her husband managed to save her on time.

Though he saved her, she still sustained sufficient amount of burns on her body. He then kept her at home, with those burns, and did not seek medical help for her. She was kept like this without medical aid for three days. Now you must understand that burns are one of the most painful conditions as they affect our skin, which has a million nerve endings, and literally she set herself on fire. Imagine a small scald or burn you have had and how much it had hurt. Now imagine a really large portion of the body burnt superficially in this manner and the person does not receive any pain medication to numb the pain.

Her son incidentally happened to mention his burnt mum's condition to a neighbour, who actually called the authorities, and that was how she ended up in front of me. I had to keep my emotions aside when I first saw her. Fear for the authorities was so great that her husband decided to ignore the pain that she was suffering. I could not comprehend how anyone could be so devoid of caring that they would allow another human being to be in so much pain with the intent to harm. That day I saw another facet of the human behaviour which I did not appreciate so much.

The Weird: All Sorts Make Up This World

I have my own demons and dark moods. It's weird.

Chris Rock

We unfortunately also get the weird and wacko stuff. Initially, I was shocked that people could do this to themselves, but later on, I accepted it in my stride that though it happens, it is not an occurrence that happens very often. Here I cannot give a graphic description as it borders on the sensational, and that is not my objective. We got to see males as well as females who presented to the emergency department with various insertions, such as glass bottles, vegetables, and even a light bulb—yes, even a light bulb.

The weird stuff does not stop there. We once had a man who came into the emergency department one early morning. He seemed fine and insisted on speaking to one of our male nurses present. Thinking that it was probably an embarrassing moment where the male patient visits the ladies of the night and seeks medical help to counter the side effects, I sent a male nurse to attend to the patient.

But it so turned out that the male nurse was embarrassed. This man who walked in came in with a plastic package in his hand. He had just been married the previous night, and he came into the ED the morning after his wedding night. Now here is where the weird stuff starts. He came over to the hospital to check if the blood staining his wife's underwear, which he put inside the package, was due to her virginity. The patient was suspicious of his wife, and he wished to verify the source of the blood! I guess all sorts of weird stuff make up this world, and in our profession, we do get to see a large percentage of the human weirdness.

The Two Sides of a Coin: Life and Death

Death is someone you see very clearly with eyes in the centre of your heart: eyes that see not by reacting to light, but by reacting to a kind of a chill from within the marrow of your own life.

Thomas Merton

I could tell you this one time when I was talking to my friend many years ago and we were doing so in the lobby area of the ED. Now my friend was a non-medical person and was a layman, not knowledgeable about medical work. As we were standing and chatting, my colleagues whizzed past us with a dead body on a trolley. Now the dead body was covered from head to foot. In those days, we did not have special trolleys to transport the patients who have passed away. Nowadays, we do have special trolleys to camouflage or shield lay people from what we see nearly every day.

My friend stopped in his tracks, and with his jaw open in shock, visibly shaken, he asked me, 'What was that?' And I, of course, told him that it was a patient who was brought in dead. My friend was shocked that I could even continue a conversation. To tell you the truth, at times specific incidents do upset us, but the sheer volume of what we go through does not give us the liberty to grieve for every single event in our professional lives. Yet I must inform you here that it does not mean that we do not respect what we face every day; we respect each and every one of our patients, whether dead or alive, and we provide privacy as well as confidentiality as our pillars of our profession. At least most of us do whisper prayers in our thoughts for peace when we are faced with situations out of the normal.

One such horrific incident is the one I have narrated below. I was visibly shaken that day, and over the years, it has remained ingrained in my heart, deep within me. You see, I had just recently lost my father, and his passing away was fresh in my mind. This was the first time after my father's death that I had come so close to a pain so immense.

One of the most painful and excruciating incidents and emotionally draining experiences which I had to deal with was a story of a thirty-five-year-old man who went home exhausted from a day's work. He had been married for about a year and worked as a foreman in the construction business. It was in the hot summer months when temperatures reached forty-five degrees and above.

He reached home sweaty and tired after a hard day of work at the docks. While he was changing his overalls, he collapsed. An ambulance was called, and he was brought to our emergency department. The first thing we did as soon as we received him was simultaneously assess the patient's breathing, and we hooked him to the cardiac monitor. We diagnosed a dying heart and tried to resuscitate him immediately. In administering adrenaline and atropine, ampoules were broken as we tried every trick in the book. Despite our aggressive resuscitative attempts, he was declared dead on arrival. Before we sent the body away to the mortuary, we waited for his family to arrive to break the awful news. We permitted the family time to come to terms with death before we transferred the body from the emergency room to the mortuary. We detached all tubes and cleaned him and made him ready for viewing by the family. While waiting for the family to arrive, we inwardly steeled ourselves and were sort of ready for the family. Yet this time around, when his family arrived, we were not prepared emotionally for the sight that greeted us.

To our utter shock, the wife was heavily pregnant with their first baby. I was pushed forward to hold the hysterical, grieving wife. I was shaking inside and was digesting this myself. I was scared, my pulse was racing, and I wrapped my arms around the wife, around her pregnant belly, to support her lest she falls down. As I had my arms around her belly, I felt the baby's kicks. I could not help it, and for once, I let the tears slide down my cheeks as I hastily swallowed the lump in my throat. It was ironic that as death stared all of us in the face, here I was feeling life in my very palms. I think it was life itself telling me that the passing away of a human life brings forth another human to be born.

The Choice to End It All

Sometimes even to live is an act of courage.

Seneca

We do get to deal with the unthinkable, mostly young adults who are frustrated with life and end it all. The suicide technique mostly chosen is by hanging themselves with a rope. The first time I witnessed it, I was shocked and shaken. Then later on, we learnt to deal with it. I did tell you earlier that we had to certify the dead bodies, and that was why this came upon us. Accompanying the physician is a nurse to assist in the examination. It was a grotesque sight to see as the rope tightly bites into the neck and the person ends up with the tongue protruding out. As we examined the body, I did think about what had driven them to do such a drastic step. I did reflect that their troubled minds were now free from misery, and I prayed that their souls find the peace that they were searching for. It is a pity that we and our patients struggle every day in hospitals as we battle to save the patients' lives, and here we have to deal with the other side of the spectrum.

Life is For Living

Never give upon someone with a
mental illness. When 'I' is replaced by
'We', illness becomes wellness.

Shannon L. Alder

This suicidal ideation brings me to the posting which is in close proximity to this, and that is psychiatry. You know, it is very difficult to see a patient who is of able body but not of sound mind. Here you get to see a patient who seems to be fine but is not. Irrelevant speeches, grandiose thoughts and ideas, and disorientation to place, person, and time are some of the signs and symptoms of these patients. Very difficult it is indeed for all—the patient, the family, and the care providers. The most painful are the addicts and the alcoholics. In the eighties, drug and alcohol rehab centres were practically non-existent, depending on which side of the globe you were on. In the absence of drug and alcohol rehab centres, the patients were forcibly admitted to the hospitals by the families to try to detoxify them—or dry them out, as it is known. But if the patient did not wish it, if the patient did not acknowledge the problem of addiction, it was a futile exercise.

These patients and their families were raged by the addiction and what it did to them. The addiction tore apart the family unit.

I knew a patient once who was an alcoholic; he was quite far gone and had developed pre-hepatic coma initially, but then he went into a hepatic coma. You see, the liver is the organ that removes all the toxins from the body, but the liver eventually succumbs to the alcohol that is pumped into the body day in and day out. This varies in degree from person to person as well as with different time frames. Now this patient was in a coma for a couple of days. At that time, I was a student nurse and did not know much about the clinical picture and the fact that eventually it could progress to a liver shut-down if one continued to drink alcohol. Now this man managed to survive the repeated episodes and came out of the coma. He physically recovered, but his mind and body were still hooked on the alcohol, for as he came out, he kept asking for a drink of alcohol. These patients do not wish to deal with their pain, and they take alcohol as a painkiller. It is a slow, painful death, and these patients would rather endure the pain from drinking too much alcohol..

In psychiatry, security and safety were always and still are a high priority for both patients and their caregivers. We receive patients with all psychiatric diagnoses, and maybe the pressure to save lives is not there, but here is another type of stress. It is our psyche that gets disturbed, and our stress levels are high. As caregivers in a psychiatric unit, we are required to always be alert and on our guard. Some of these patients could potentially harm themselves or others. Reasoning with them is most of the time laborious, and you need heaps of patience. We have had many circumstances in psychiatric units where small fires were started, patients attempted suicides, as well as patients absconding from the unit. What we manage to provide inside hospitals would only cover a fraction of what the patient or family endures at home or in the community.

It is disturbing to witness how at times we had to resort to physically restraining the patient if our other methods were not successful. Equally stressful for us was to assist patients through the shock therapy. When I started my career, this was often administered to patients. It entails a small electric current being administered by which the patient goes into a convulsive state and then for some time into a daze. When the patient comes around, they are confused, disoriented, and dishevelled, with spittle drooling from their mouths. It is really heartbreaking to see this happen to our patients. I am sure you must have seen the process sometime in a film, and it did seem barbaric to me at that time. Thankfully, this practice is not the preferred line of treatment now and is rarely administered. Psychiatry has evolved tremendously, and another branch of it that is psychology has made progress by leaps and bounds. The stigma attached to psychiatry and psychology has lessened over the years, and now we see positive influence in the community.

Obsessed

Nobody can hurt me without my permission.

Mahatma Gandhi

The story I am about to tell you is one about a permanent necklace that a girlfriend received from her so-called boyfriend. Unusually, the emergency department was quiet that day. It was around four in the afternoon. I had just come on the afternoon shift. We were settling down to a peaceful shift when the emergency bell was rung. In those days, the notification system had not yet evolved, so all we were informed of was that a trauma patient was on the way. The actual description of the trauma case eluded us, so we prepared for the worst, hoping that it would not be so bad.

We went to receive the patient, and the scene that met our eyes seemed unreal. A young lady in her early thirties, clad in cream-coloured horse-riding gear, was lying down on the ambulance trolley. From afar, she seemed fine, conscious, but on examining her closely, we found that her throat was slit. We could see her pulsating jugular, missed by a millimetre.

The girl volunteered the information that it was indeed her boyfriend who gave her this necklace.

You see, the girlfriend was an outgoing, socially extroverted girl, much to the dismay of her overly jealous boyfriend. Many a time, fights broke out between them as the issue was disliked by the boyfriend.

That day the girlfriend was horse riding against her boyfriend's wishes, and he approached her and told her to stop. This led to an argument, and the boyfriend became physically abusive with her. In a flash of a few seconds, the girlfriend found her throat was slit by her boyfriend. And she was rushed to the emergency department.

As we proceeded to prepare her for surgery, she told me, 'He loves me so much.' I was shocked that I actually witnessed what we only usually see in movies or read about in the novels, not in real life. On that day, I learnt a valuable lesson. All I know is that love only loves; it does not hurt. I also got to know the many facets of so-called love which we permit.

Miracles Are Just around the Corner

Faith is the first factor in a life devoted to
service. Without it, nothing is possible.
With it, nothing is impossible.

Mary McLeod Bethune

I met her parents while she was in a coma. The
coma was an outcome of tuberculous meningitis,
which is caused by *Mycobacterium tuberculosis*.
The meninges are the system of membranes which
envelops the central nervous system, and this is the
most common form of CNS tuberculosis. This is when
you get tuberculosis (or TB in layman's terminology),
which affects your brain.

She was in a coma for a very long time. From
a teenager of sixteen, she was transformed into a
lifeless person with a tube sticking out of her mouth
as she was hooked on to a life support machine. Her
parents were by her side, frequently praying and
holding on to a glimmer of hope. I was informed by
a common friend who requested me to visit her and
her parents as she lay in the ICU. At that time, I had
just started working in a female medical ward, so one
day on my lunch break, I decided to meet the parents

and convey my friend's regards. You see, as staff working in a hospital, we often get these personal requests and do definitely oblige.

On meeting them, I was pleasantly surprised to see very easy-going parents, scared but strong in their hope and conviction. I stayed for a few minutes and nearly went every day to the ICU to pay them a visit. The coma lasted for three weeks. For her parents, it seemed like eternity.

Eventually, this young girl pulled through. She was weaned away from the ventilator and was extubated, and she made it on her own, initially breathing oxygen through a nasal cannula, which delivered the oxygen, and then was finally able to survive on room air. Oxygen saturation was about 94 per cent, and all her vital signs were stable, so she was fit to be transferred out to a ward. As luck would have it, she was transferred to my unit. Her family and I became very good friends.

Then came the painstaking work we and the patient had to put in so she could regain her healthy status. She had to make her body relearn everything she had forgotten. For starters, the first task was toilet training. She was still on the urinary catheter, and we had to clamp it hourly to train her to feel the urge to urinate, and then we would release the clamps. We had to teach her to walk with intensive physical therapy. To my delight, I discovered she was a bubbly, positive girl, and we kept her preoccupied with jokes and anecdotes. We kept her company through her long hospital stay, spending hours after we completed all our assignments. We usually dimmed the lights at around nine at night, and once we documented the shift's notes and completed all our assigned patient care, we did go to spend time with her. With all the determination in this world, she made it, regaining all she had lost before the event and making a fabulous full recovery.

She is one of the few patients I did meet after her discharge from the hospital to see her happily married and well settled.

A Lifetime of Remorse and Guilt

Nothing is more wretched than the
mind of a man conscious of guilt.

Plautus

It was on a weekday, at around 07.30. We had only just started our morning shift. Suddenly, ambulance sirens screeched outside the ED doors. The shrill shriek of the emergency bell was heard, and we rushed to bring in a casualty. It was a young woman dressed in office-going attire, pale-pink skirt, and jacket suit. She was badly injured in a horrific road traffic accident. For the next two hours, we desperately tried to revive her broken body. She had suffered massive internal injuries, and all our resuscitative attempts were futile; she finally succumbed to the injuries, and we reluctantly had to declare her dead. It is at times like these that we have to deal with our own feelings and had to come to terms with the finality of the outcome. So heaviness was in our hearts that we had not saved her, and we had to let her go.

In came her distraught husband with two small kids. It seems the kids had missed their school bus, and it was exam time. The husband decided to escort the kids to school as well as take his wife to work before taking himself to work. Apparently, he was speeding as they were already late. A U-turn taken hastily ended it all for them as there was an oncoming truck that collided with his car.

He was completely lost and broken when he was told that his wife was no more. The physician who broke the news to him did so devoid of emotion, and my heart went out to him.

I approached him to comfort him with a few words. He wished me to walk with him in his darkest pain. The next few moments were especially tender; he was alone with his thoughts but was speaking them aloud to me. He needed somebody to hear him out, somebody neutral who would not judge him, and I was chosen for that special moment. I could see that he was weary with pain, though he seemed outwardly calm. He told me of his deep love for her. He then removed his wallet to show me his wife's picture. I could see a fun-loving person through the photograph he showed me. The circumstances in which they got married were marred with disapproval as she got married to him without her parents' permission. All he felt was the tremendous burden of guilt. He was afraid of the future, how he would explain to her parents that he was behind the wheel and that he was responsible for her passing away. He was fearful of the future for his school going boys. This conversation lasted not more than ten minutes but had a great impact on me. I do hope that by my listening to him that early morning, I managed to impart solace and strength to his troubled heart.

A Woman's Dignity

Only the weak are cruel. Gentleness can
only be expected from the strong.

Leo Buscaglia

It was the night shift. We were fairly busy, and I was stationed in the obstetrics and gynaecology unit. No patient was in labour, so it would be a light night. Around two in the morning, we received a young lady in her early twenties. She was in pain and frightened like a small caged animal. You could see that she was just married as she had presented to the hospital in all her bridal finery.

She did not say anything at all to us. Her husband did the talking. It was their wedding night. It seemed that he had consummated the marriage, and now the lady was bleeding. The female gynaecologists and I proceeded to examine her, but the patient was so tense and frightened that she would not permit us to examine her. At that moment, following the gynaecologists advise I reinforced external packs in an attempt to arrest bleeding. The patient was sent home with her husband and was informed to observe the bleeding.

Now I was about twenty-two years old and could not fully comprehend the extent to what had happened. So I momentarily threw it out of my mind, and I proceeded to relax for the rest of the night. But the patient returned around four in the early morning, still profusely bleeding.

The gynaecologist who saw her earlier was summoned by me. The patient and her husband were then informed that an examination under general anaesthesia could be conducted to see what the problem was. The required documents were consented after a detailed explanation, and the lady was taken into the operating theatre.

Soon after that, it became clear what the issue was. It seems it was an arranged marriage, and the bride was not ready for the physical aspects of the marriage. She was frightened of the impending act of consummation. She voiced her fears to the husband, who was impatient and would not wait. As she was very tense, she was not relaxed and resisted his advances, and this resulted in a second-degree tear, which had to be repaired under anaesthesia. This event shook my core as a woman and our weakness at the mercy of a ruthless, uncaring man. With the increase in violent crimes targeted at women, what about the crimes which are taking place within the sanctity of marriage?

Tragedy Strikes

It is not the length of life, but the depth of life.

Ralph Waldo Emerson

He was a patient in our hospital for over two months. He had suffered a cerebral vascular accident, known commonly as a stroke. He served his family well, and in order to do that, he had left his home country. He had gone far away from the family for twenty-four years to earn his daily bread in order to keep the home fires burning. While working away from his family, stress had the better of him, and he suffered diabetes and hypertension. Like *married bachelors*, a term given to married men who live far away from their home countries as singles, unhealthy eating and drinking habits were part of his daily routine.

Now with the stroke, he was incapacitated, and he was under physical rehabilitation. So not long after the stroke, a joint decision by the company had been made with the patient's consent that he could opt out for voluntary retirement. Now, he was working for a multinational company, so the company was kind enough to ensure that his wife could come to assist him tie up the loose ends. He needed help to pack off all his belongings as he would say adieu to his second home of many years.

The wife arrived eventually and took over his paperwork instantly. She got into action, acquiring a wheelchair for him so that he could be mobile with ease. In a matter of a couple of days after she arrived, she felt unwell. The nurses who were taking care of her husband guided her to arrive at the emergency department.

And that was how I met her. I was assigned in the triage when I met her. *Triage* is the term that is given for a quick assessment which is done at the point of entry to the emergency department. Triage is done to prioritize patient care into emergent and non-emergent based on predetermined criteria. It is done so that we do not miss the patients that need our utmost care in the quickest time possible.

She had some vague complains. Her jaw seemed stuck, and she was having difficulty with the stiffness; she was experiencing difficulty while closing it. Unlike a patient with a dislocated jaw, who cannot close the jaw, she could still close her jaw. On probing and questioning her further, we found out that she had a rusty-nail injury on her foot before departing from her home country. In her hurry to meet her husband with all that she had to get done, she had not taken the recommended tetanus toxoid injections, which are vital for all cuts, bites, bruises, lacerations, and nail injuries.

She had contracted nasty tetanus. Brave attempts were made to save her, but it resulted in a negative outcome. And in just over a couple of days, the unthinkable happened. The wife who had come to escort and assist the wheelchair-bound husband was herself found to be departing in a casket, cold and still.

Not Yours to Nurture, Oh Mother

Faith consists in believing when it is beyond
the power of reason to believe.

Voltaire

We bottle-fed the infant babies in front of their natural mothers, and they were not even aware that these were their babies.

How was this even possible, that the baby being fed in my arms was hers and yet she was not even aware that it was hers? Did I steal this baby or kidnap it? Or was the mother suffering from some psychiatric illness that prevented her from recognizing this baby? These are sure some of the questions that came up in your mind as you read my earlier remarks. It is life's twists and turns. Life's horrible truth will be told.

It is about teenagers with unwanted pregnancies, wild parties, peer pressure, and so on—rebellious teenagers who did not comprehend the consequences or outcomes of their actions. For a short period, I worked in a hospital organization as a volunteer which was a shelter of some sorts, a shelter for these unwed mothers who were very tender in their age. The way the system operated was, the expectant mother was welcomed to stay in the organization until the birth of the baby and eventually the baby was put up for adoption. The expectant mother had to be a minor below sixteen years of age and her parent or guardian had to sign and admit her in the hospital and consent to all the necessary legal paperwork that went with it. It worked well for the family of the expectant mother who would otherwise have to hang their heads in shame. In the late eighties, unwed young expectant mothers brought shame to their family and were ostracized by the society they lived in. The social stigma was huge; you could not even discuss it in public.

Yet I feel the unwed expectant mother was not taken into consideration. There seemed to be no counselling provided, especially as the victim was a minor. Everything seemed to be hushed up, and we who worked there were not allowed to query about anything. All expenses of the expectant mother and her soon to-be-born baby were paid for by the couple adopting the baby. The family of the expectant mother did not bear any of the expenses even if the expectant mother stayed in the hospital for over six months at a stretch.

One such girl had come in advanced pregnancy at the age of fourteen. Initially, the mother of the young expectant girl thought that the extra weight that the young girl was putting on was just a result of growth spurt. Additionally, her missed monthly periods were also thought to be irregularity of initial periods by her mother as physiologically it sometimes does happen. By the time the pregnancy was discovered, it was too long gone to have a medical termination of the pregnancy. Supposedly, her tuition master had taken advantage of her. The father of this young girl was in the Gulf, and the mother was all alone taking care of her. The family did not intend to fight it out as it would bring a lot of unnecessary media attention upon them. All this was narrated to me by the worried mother of the young girl.

And so this young petite girl ended up being our companion for the next few months. She was happily unaware of what had befallen her and would bounce around the long corridors of the hospital, big tummy and all. She was still in school, and I recall that she went for her exams from the hospital.

In school, when the big tummy was noticed, she was made to sit by herself for the first exam. The school finally exempted her for all the remaining examinations and avoided future embarrassment. The school took it upon themselves to promote her to the next standard after the dreadful episode would be over.

Months went by where we would have long chats with this young girl, but we were instructed that we could not ask her any personal questions. As she had time on her hands, she played games with us, ate with us, and generally was part of our unit. Soon the time for her delivery came nearer, and I was worried for her. She was oblivious to pain that would come her way. Thankfully, I was not on duty when she went into labour. I met her a day after the delivery. After the delivery, she metamorphosed from a fun-loving child into a quiet, pained adult at the age of fourteen. Her eyes told me the amount of pain that she had just endured. I never had the courage to ask her about her pain as at that time I had no answers, being only a few years older than her fourteen years.

She was allowed to see the baby only once through hazy eyes during delivery when she was under sedation. She could not register the baby's face, and after the delivery, she was administered medications so her milk was chemically induced to dry.

That was how my heart raced—I had this big, huge secret in my heart—when I fed her baby in front of her and she was very quiet by my side. We were never going to discuss the identity of the babies in our arms. For me, it was a very sad feeling; I held their babies in my arms, yet they were not even allowed to hold their own babies. For me, that opened my eyes in a different way altogether.

Angel in the Sky

One word frees us of all the weight
and pain of life: That word is love.

Sophocles

The pain of seeing your loved one suffer is unbearable, especially if that loved one is your child. It cannot be measured but can be felt deep down in your core. There was this little young girl who was bubbly in nature, always happy and cheerful. After a bout of flu, coupled with lethargy and some vague symptoms, she was diagnosed with leukaemia. This news devastated the family. Now the family was a middle-class family with not much financial security. The mother of this girl was a working mother who strived for the best for the family.

Simultaneously, the little girl's grandmother, who was a diabetic, deteriorated and got renal failure. The grandmother was put on renal haemodialysis, which means in simple language 'mechanically doing the job of the kidneys' in order to sustain life. Now I am not sure if you know the gravity of the situation, but renal failure by itself can be painful to accept. The mother of this young girl had to alternate between cycles of chemotherapy and dialysis. This was extremely stressful, but that was how it was for the months that followed.

I remember a time when the mother was distraught as her little girl was ill when her blood counts were at an all-time low and the grandmother had constipation for at least a week. She then visited the hospital with the grandmother, and I gently performed manual faecal removal. No matter how gently we try to be, as the stool is hard, it turns out to be painfully stressful for the patients. The procedure requires you to wear gloves and be as gentle as possible while you insert your fingers to remove stool manually. Eventually, as you remove the stool and the bowel is empty, the patient does get relief. We do administer some painkillers before we attempt the procedure as the patient is weak, chronically sick, and the ensuing pain may stress them even more.

Anyways, let's go back to the little girl's story as it is this little girl that I wish to focus on. I did not administer clinical care for her, but as the grandmother was my patient, I got to meet and know her. She was a pretty girl, with fair complexion and light-green eyes. Seeing her initially, you would not know that she was suffering from leukaemia. The mother was pained to see the girl wasting away with the leukaemia day by day. Sadly, the girl did not respond to the treatment provided, and she became terminal. Though I did not administer direct care to the girl as a nurse, I knew the family and did visit the girl and kept in touch with the family.

The day came when the girl was critical; she did lose her consciousness but was still alive and struggling. Her mother sat continuously by her side. Now for this mother, she was her only daughter— though she had a son too, who was the older sibling. After a couple of days of struggle in the ICU, the oncologist (a doctor who is specialized in cancer care) and the intensivist did approach the mother, and she was given counselling. She was told that her daughter was barely alive and holding on to this world, but the mother was not ready to let the little one go. They explained that the daughter, though she was in a coma, sensed that the mother was in turmoil. Now you must know that the physicians, especially oncologists, do witness tragedies nearly every single day. They have strong intuition, which others cannot fathom.

The mother was taken aside and told to let her go, that her daughter was holding on because of her. Finally, the mother understood that this was the end. She composed herself, went into a corner, and prayed for a long time. She pleaded with God to give her the strength to deal with the pain of it all. The mother was weary, tired, and just wished to rest. She emerged more peaceful and serene. Armed with this serenity and peace, she went beside her daughter. She held her little daughter's hands and silently cried tears, tears of gratitude that she had enjoyed her daughter's life even if it was short-lived, and tears of pain, tears of agony in knowing what was to come upon them. And yet she did what she knew she had to do. The mother was ready to let go, wept, and sobbed her heart out. While she was still holding her daughter's hands, her daughter's life slipped away.

She became an angel, and the mother had her strength to carry on with her memories.

I Count My Blessings

Life is a succession of lessons which
must be lived to be understood.

Helen Keller

She was a petite lady who approached me as I was preparing to go to the staff cafeteria to catch a quick lunch. She first asked me for a lady police constable. Her eyes were brimming with tears. I knew that whatever was troubling her was a very difficult situation. Though lunch was on my mind, then and there I decided lunch could wait, and I proceeded to hear her out. I then asked her what her problem was, and she broke down. Between sobs, she managed to tell me that she was beaten by her husband.

She was afraid, shivering maybe with the chill in the air, but I put it down to fear. With no parents and no family to fall back on, she was lonely. She was a housewife and was not financially secure and independent while her husband was established, rich, and had connections with the right people. She wanted to register a police case in case it got ugly and wanted it for record purposes. She had no other alternative but to go back to the same house for the sake of her children, who were still toddlers.

Once I assisted her to meet the physician and the police, I had to leave her helpless in her situation. As I walked towards the staff canteen, my mood was pensive, lost in my thoughts yet with gratitude in my heart for not being in the same dilemma.

Shroud to Cover Thy Body

Those who have the strength and the love
to sit with a dying patient in the silence that
goes beyond words will know that this moment
is neither frightening nor painful, but a peaceful
cessation of the functioning of the body.

Elisabeth Kübler-Ross

I met them in the busy and bustling ED. He was an old man, probably over eighty. He was wrinkled and bent over. But his eyes burnt with brilliance. It was his eyes that attracted me, that beckoned me. They were seated just outside the resuscitation rooms, on benches provided to families of critical patients. It meant that someone who belonged to them was inside, fighting for life. I was already off my shift and was actually on my way home. So I did go over to offer a cup of warm beverage. It turned out that the old man's wife was inside our resuscitation room.

I sat and chatted with the weary old man. He then opened up to me. You know, at your most vulnerable moments, you wish to hold someone's hand, someone to hear you out, so I presented myself. This is their story.

They had been married together for over sixty years. He took me into his past, I think, urged by the strong emotion to tell someone else that he deeply loved her. It was Nineteen Hundred and Fifty and they had a romantic beginning. Both had run away from their respective homes to be together. They came from different religious backgrounds, and the social strata prevalent then would not permit their union. In the good old days, this eloping was unheard off. Along with him, I did meet his daughter and son-in-law, who were by his side at all times. He was never left alone. It never fails to warm my heart to see families supporting each other at times like this. It is in moments devoid of glamour and glitz that you know who your family is.

Over the next few days, I kept in touch, drawn to them like a magnet. I could see despair tearing away their souls. I was somehow connected to them through the recesses of our souls. I am not sure, but through all the medical jargon that was thrown at them, I gave their hearts some solace and warmth. You could see a love and humility in their hearts that was difficult for me to ignore.

The wife and mother was attached to a ventilator, and you knew how difficult it was for the family to see their mother amongst all these tubes. The rhythmic whirring of the machines reminded them of the stark reality of the pain that befalls them. The grim reality of the ICU, pain all around them, patients who were critically sick, and patients who were in deep coma disturbed them.

After a couple of days of struggle, his wife did pass away. I was there throughout their ordeal.

Knowing the painful process ahead for them, I did offer to be there for them. I enquired if they had any family member who could help them to dress up their mother before she started on her final journey. And on hearing that no one would be present with them, I decided to be part of their family in this very intimate moment. It was a touching and emotional day for me as the old baba was there and so was his daughter. Though many a time before I have participated in this ritual, it was the first time that I did so while not on duty. It was also the first time I did so in a mortuary. It was very emotional for me. I understood their pain, became one with them.

As we proceeded to bathe and dress her up, we silently cried, and we whispered our prayers in our hearts. The daughter spoke to her mama, holding her frail father and giving him strength that he so needed. His soulmate was leaving him alone after being there together for many, many years. The daughter and the old baba were in so much of pain as they dressed her up in the colours mama liked and sprayed her with the perfume that she adored. For me, this is love—not only when you buy red roses on Valentine's Day, but that you are there to bid your goodbye with as much grace as you can muster.

I had willingly offered to do this though I knew it would take a toll on me. Yet it has enriched my life, to celebrate a woman's life and death and be part of the family. Ironically, it was on International Women's Day when we sent her on her final journey. I am proud of the fact that I honoured a woman of substance today. I am writing this on the very same day, and I am still lost somewhere in my thoughts.

Like they say in Urdu, 'Jannat Ki Havaa, Maa Ki Duaa'. In translation, it means 'A breeze from heaven can be found in a mother's blessings'!

Faith and Prayer Alone Can . . .

Prayer is the key of the morning
and the bolt of the evening.

Mahatma Gandhi

It was just around 04.15 on a quiet and still night. There were not many patients coming to the ED. A bunch of us were sitting around, sipping mugs of hot coffee. The sharp shrill of an emergency bell broke that silence. Two of us rushed out to check the alarm bell. We saw a private vehicle driven by a middle-aged man. An older hunchbacked lady was sitting in the front passenger seat. A young girl was found lying in the back seat of their car. They did tell us that the young girl was unwell, so we proceeded to take her out of the car. She must have been around sixteen years of age. She seemed to be in a deep sleep, not rousable, as we tried to wake her up when we were removing her out of the car. So we ran as fast as we could with her atop a trolley to our resuscitation rooms. We were informed that the relatives were the patient's father and grandmother. We closed the doors of the resuscitation room and proceeded to cut her clothes and connect her to our cardiac monitor. During emergencies, it is all hands on deck. We work with speed but with precision.

What followed after that has forever been imprinted on my soul. The cardiac monitor showed us a straight line (*asystole* in medical terms). We were all shocked and did our level best to save her life. But this young life had passed, and we were futile in our attempts.

We then had the very difficult job of breaking the news to the family. We found out that this girl had been unwell with a fever for three days, for which she had visited a family physician, and was prescribed medication by the family physician. This particular night, she was sleeping with her grandmother. According to the grandmother, in the middle of the night, the grandmother heard some grunting. Hearing the grunting, the grandmother woke up from her slumber. She turned to look at her granddaughter. As the grandmother found her granddaughter was looking ashen, she tried to wake her up. When the grandmother was not successful in waking up the granddaughter, she alerted her son, the father of the young girl, and they brought her to the hospital.

The physician did explain to the family and gave them the bad news. We were prepared for screams and a hysterical reaction from both the father as well as the grandmother. We got no screams and loud cries, but we did get a silent shocked reaction, with tears streaming down their faces. The father shortly left the emergency department. Now you must understand that it was eerily silent in the night. All the neighbouring areas adjacent to the emergency department were still and quiet, not operational in the night. The units were open and bustling with activity only in the morning.

As the father left the ED, I was curious and wanted to know where he was going after we gave him such terrible news. I also wanted to know how he was so calm even in the face of his worst nightmare. I followed him without letting him know I was following him. I am glad that the curiosity got the better of me that day, for what I saw that night has changed me. He went into some of the lost dark corridors of the hospital, and then when he found a quiet corner, he went down on his knees and started to pray. At that magical moment, everything became still for me. I was in awe, and I waited only for a moment, lost in prayer with him. I left him alone with his solace and serenity and took away with me my serenity.

Feel-Good Factor

May you live all the days of your life.

Jonathan Swift

On days that I am particularly down and upset, going to work is the best option. There is no better way than coming to work and going through our reality checks. The hospital is a place that keeps me grounded like nothing else.

Just meeting patients that cross my path pulls me out of my own depressing thoughts. Even simple events, such as telling a seventeen-year-old that he or she has been diagnosed with juvenile diabetes or seeing a cerebral palsy child who is also epileptic and has become a crisis for a family, can be crushing that you tend to forget your own misery. For us, it could be simple, but for the patient and the patient's family, the message that we convey can be devastating. With this devastation, we have to assure our patients and hope with them. In doing so, we assure ourselves and hope for ourselves. It is a circle of hope in life. This reminds me of our own fragility. In the process, my heart receives solace.

I must tell you what I do when I feel that my problems are too much to handle and feel like I have the whole world on my shoulders. I go to the beach. The ocean always calms me. The vastness and depth of the ocean brings for me tranquillity.

For me, circumstances and situations that are presented to me speak volumes. I learn continuously. I consciously remember my awe moments, and I count my blessings. With all its ups and downs, life is worth living.

I Wished for Shoes Until . . .

Certain thoughts are prayers.
There are moments when, whatever be
the attitude of the body, the soul is on its knees.

Victor Hugo

The ambulance informed us that a trauma casualty was on the way to our emergency department. One by one we were taking time off for lunch. For us, there is no specific time slot for us to take our breaks; we take it whenever the patient load is light. At times, we do not even get time to grab a bite. I decided to wait and assist with this patient. I knew that maybe a polytrauma protocol would be announced. A polytrauma code is alerted when a critical trauma patient arrives in the ED. With this announcement, a whole bunch of specialists will descend on the ED to assist with the care.

The patient was brought in, and we saw that he was critical. A polytrauma code was announced. The patient was conscious and told us that he works in the docks. They were unloading large heavy metal sheets. He was standing far away from the loading bay. It was a hot windy day with a sandstorm and great, gusty winds. According to him, he did not know how, but one of the metal sheets came unhooked from the loading truck. This heavy metal sheet flew towards him and sliced off both his feet within a few seconds. Now I have seen many trauma patients—it is my job, like it is yours to pore over papers and such. What has touched me is that this particular patient was fasting for a religious reason. He was calm and accepted his condition, knowing fully well what had happened to him. In fact, he did actually tell me that God is our maker and we should surrender our selves to the will of God. Initially, the moment that I had seen what my patient had undergone, my faith was shaken, but on seeing his immense faith and surrender, the patient himself gave me back my faith. In hospitals, if we keep all our senses alert, we get to witness miracles of human faith continuously.

All Our Senses

Just because a man lacks the use of his
eyes doesn't mean he lacks vision.

Stevie Wonder

Talking about our senses, I remember this one event which brings to my mind how we take our senses for granted.

We take turns to work on the weekend, as it is not desirable for us to work on the weekend. We rotate the weekend offs, so that all of us get this privilege. We have a process where we can request for an off as well as we can swap our shifts with another colleague. We just ought to make sure that the skill mix and the seniority are maintained. On one such weekend morning, I did not wish to be on duty and was reluctantly in the hospital. This is one day that I wished to be off. Anyways, let us go back to the weekend morning. It was a lazy, quiet morning. It was also a cold winter morning, and temperatures do dip low.

We received a patient who had gone dune-bashing in the deserts. While driving in the dunes, this strapping young male adult in his early twenties met an accident. Now it was not a catastrophic accident, but what happened to him that morning changed his life forever. While manoeuvring a dune on the way down, he lost control of the vehicle. The vehicle turned turtle on him, and somersaulted out of control. As he met with the accident, his face hit the dashboard, with his chin making contact on impact. This particular action proved disastrous for him. In medical terminology, we call it mechanism of injury. As the chin hit the dashboard, the impact forced both his eyeballs out from his eye sockets. So when we received him, we were horrified to notice that both his eyeballs were out, with his optic nerves severed. The eyeballs were still bandaged to his face, but they were not connected to his face any more. The patient was not told what had happened to him.

We did request for expert opinion from a travelling group of eye surgeons, but the verdict was negative in his favour as the optic nerves were destroyed. I have never seen this again in all my years of working with trauma, and my core was shocked that this young patient lost his eyesight in a flash of a moment on that weekend morning. The patient was sedated in the emergency room so that he did not have to deal with the immediate painful truth.

I have included this story so that you can be shocked as I was on that day and not take anything for granted. Every now and then, if I tend to forget this, I get reminded through my experiences that life is too short and our peace is only in our moments and our serenity is in these present moments. And now I know why I was supposed to work on that particular weekend.

The Nightmare of a Holiday

The life of the dead is placed in
the memory of the living.

Marcus Tullius Cicero

It was the region's religious feast. Along with the weekend, about four days of public holidays were declared. Though the region's offices were shut, those are the days we were normally very busy in the ED. Since holidays were declared, most of the people try to travel out of the station. For those that are not travelling to exotic locations, the option left is to travel within and outside the city limits. So we get busy with many accidents even though the public is warned to stay safe on the roads.

Initially, the public holiday starts with being quiet in the morning, but as the day wears on, we start getting busy as people hit the roads. When we start the day, we do so with a whisper of prayer in our hearts to keep everyone safe. So on this holiday, in the early afternoon, we got a call that we would be receiving a road traffic accident by helicopter.

You see, we had a helipad attached to our hospital to receive critical patients who needed to be airlifted. We went out to receive this patient; in fact, we rushed to the helipad as we did not get much warning, and we heard the whirring of the helicopter blades approaching. It was a hot offloading, which meant that we approached the helicopter with caution as the helicopter motor blades are still on. The patient was rushed to the resuscitation room. She was a front-seat occupant in a car accident. It seemed like she was in her early forties. We fought to keep her alive, but her injuries were extensive, and we lost her. Her relatives had not yet reached our emergency department, so presently, though she was declared as a death in the department, we could not address any of our formalities of packing up the body as we usually wait for the near and dear ones to reach and we try to give them some sort of closure. So we patiently waited and cleaned her up and removed all bloody marks and tubes as best as we could to make her presentable.

We shortly received her relatives. A pair of teenagers, a brother and a sister maybe sixteen and seventeen years old, came in, frantic for news of her. With them was also a young male adult about twenty-one years old or so. We found out that these were her children. We had to break the news as gently as possible because we learnt that just two years ago, the family had lost their ailing father. Yet we were not prepared for the aftermath of our news. All pandemonium broke loose when we told them that their mother had passed away. The elder son started crying hysterically and screaming, 'I killed my mother, I killed my mother.' He kept screaming and repeating the same thing over and over again.

He was beyond control, and we had to leave him to grieve.

The teenage children were still in shock and did not know how to react. They told us that their elder brother had just got his driving licence and decided to take the mother, his brother, and sister for a spin. They rented a car and went for a drive. The son was speeding, and the car somersaulted out of control.

Only the mother had severe injuries; her children were safe. The pain of this event is still fresh in my mind, their shocked expressions forever embedded in my memory. A moment can change our lives, and we would have to live with it.

Disclosure

Human salvation demands the divine
disclosure of truths surpassing reason.

Thomas Aquinas

What is *disclosure*? The dictionary meaning
states that it is 'to make known or to
expose'. But here I mean it in the context of patient
information, particularly the diagnosis and the
prognosis or an outcome of the diseased condition.
In certain countries, patient information is governed
by law, and in certain countries, it is subjectively used
by the medical fraternity.

It is difficult for patients and their families to
disguise their fears. They put their lives in our hands—
to engage them, to allay away their fears, to soothe
their worries, to sometimes prepare them for the
inevitable. We become their source of information,
their guide and advocate.

I do know at times we—or at least, some of us—
do not like to hear what is being told. Some of us
have an inner strength; though we do not like to
hear what is being told, we can still brave it out
there. The patient's world in hospitals is scary, dark;
looming ahead is fear of the unknown. Patients and

their families have to walk on unchartered pathways, sometimes alone.

In my capacity as a nurse, I prefer the advocacy of truth, disclosing information that is within the patient's right to have access to the medical information. After all, it is the patient's life. I do gauge and assess my patients and their families' capacity to accept the truth. I prefer to tell them as gently as possible but tell them as it is. I lost my father at a very young age, and there were so many things left unsaid that if I could, I would prevent the same for my patients and families.

Disclosing a patient's diagnosis or the prognosis is very difficult; it is a very thin line to cross as we are not sure how much of the gravity or intensity we should disclose. Is there hope? Have we, as the healers, lost all hope? Are we doing our best with all the medical expertise and resources available? Sometimes anger from patients and their families do confront us. They put us in a quandary as experience tells us something else.

I do strongly believe that if the days ahead are going to be painful, the patient's families have each other. They can derive strength from each other. The patient knows that in his passing away, his family has made peace. Love and strength are their pillars to carry on his legacy and values. The love that the patient has sown will last a lifetime; the patient lives on through the family, etched in their memories forever, and this will be passed on.

As nurses, we are very adept at camouflaging our emotions in front of our patients. Unfortunately, we may seem a bit stoic at times to others, but it is a learnt practice to appear strong. It is when you see how very painful it sometimes is, seeing grown men sob with anguish, that it tears at your heart. It is a tough job, and we undertake it and accomplish it with pride.

My Awe Moments

There are in life a few moments so beautiful,
that even words are a sort of profanity.

Diana Palmer

I have had several awe moments in this nursing career. Sometimes your mouth is left wide open at the stark reality of what unfolds before you. In nursing, it is one step further, wherein your heart and mouth are both shocked and are at a standstill. One of the biggest joys I have experienced is witnessing the birth of life, and this joy becomes greater when I do get an opportunity to assist in this phenomena. No matter how much we studied in structured classrooms, the sheer miracle of life happening in front of our eyes was something else.

The atmosphere in a delivery room is one charged with a whole range of emotions, depending on how smooth the actual delivery is. Is it regarded as a normal delivery or a special, precious birth? Is it a premature birth? Are the mother's and baby's lives in danger? As the baby's head crowns, the joy of the mystery of life unfolding before your eyes cannot be described into words. I actually believe nothing could surpass the miracle of life during birth.

Talking about precious births and deliveries, I must retell the story of this young mother who had an incompetent Os. Now let me just explain that the cervix has an opening called Os, which is tightly sealed during the nine months of the pregnancy and opens only in preparation for birth. This opening up of the cervix is what we actually refer to as the dilatation during labour. Now this particular patient had an incompetent Os, which meant it recurrently opened during the pregnancy as the pregnancy advanced. As a matter of fact, if the Os starts dilating, you could end up going through labour and having a premature delivery of your baby. By the time I met her, she had had seven premature births, and none of her babies had survived the ordeal. This was her eighth pregnancy, and she was administered the Shirodkar stitch, which is a procedure done to prevent the Os from opening. The amazing bit of this story is that though this patient once again had a premature delivery, this time the baby survived— though being only 700 grams at birth. So for me, witnessing the mother's torture and having the baby make it through this ordeal were nothing short of an awe moment.

Babies with meconium aspiration survive after weeks of being in the NICU or the neonatal ICU. *Meconium* is the very first stool of a neonate, which happens soon after the baby is born. Sometimes during a stressful labour, if the foetus cannot handle the stress and strain of the delivery, it will pass this meconium inside the uterus and thus the foetus aspirates the contaminated fluid. This could lead to a string of complications for the newborn baby, and once again as nurses, we are delighted when one such baby makes it home safe and sound.

But I was yet to witness the miracle of a patient defying death against all odds and surviving it all. The rare occurrence of this phenomenon for me was my super awe moment and one that I would cherish for all time. Especially the times when we are resuscitating one of our critical patients and during the resuscitation the patient pulls through or when we are administering electric shocks to the heart and hoping against hope that the rhythm on the cardiac monitor changes to a sinus rhythm, which is a normal cardiac rhythm, that for me is an ultimate super awe moment.

The other awe moments are patients pulling out of a coma and making significant recovery. Seeing patients making steady improvements after spinal surgeries or orthopaedic surgeries and actually seeing them walk are like witnessing a baby taking his first steps in life. The numerous cancer survivors, the asthmatics and the many trauma patients who are discharged home after months of being hospitalised simply brings a cheer to my heart. By nature, most of us are positive people; we ought to be if we are to instil hope in others.

The following are not actually awe moments, but they do come under the category of special, tender moments that tell us our job is the most satisfying one on a Richter scale of human emotions.

Now I shall just let you imagine this. The patient has just had a cervical injury. The spinal column at the neck level is called the cervical spine. Bony injuries or fractures sustained in this area pose a very serious risk that the patient could become a quadriplegic patient. For cervical injuries, we maintain cervical immobilization, which entails ensuring the neck area is kept still and does not move. The principle in treatment is not to mobilize an injured spine and aggravate the injury further. Quadriplegia means that this patient will be unable to move any of his limbs below the neck level. Imagine if your mind is active but your body keeps you a prisoner. It will be a living nightmare for you. The condition poses a lot of complications from this immobilization for such a patient. We do put the quadriplegic patient on a Stryker bed, which provides traction for the spine and attempts to correct the spinal injury. Just providing a warm cup of tea, spending time with, and reassuring such a patient brings solace to my heart and tells me that our lives are so fragile.

Specially tender moments for me are also when each one of our patients leaves the hospital; we are saddened as we had got used to them and their strength. They suffered in silence and were never once unkind to us. We miss them sitting in their chair or bed, silently watching us from the corner of their eyes. Their farewell is bittersweet—bitter because they were not amongst us any more and sweet as we know they were at peace now, either discharged hale and hearty at home with their loved ones if they were blessed to have that or at peace forever in a permanent resting place.

In the next half hour, someone else will take their corner, and someone else will fill our lives with chores and emotions. I am prepared to learn from the next patient lessons of diseased conditions but supplemented with lessons of life. Every day we learn something new as each patient teaches us something new, however minute.

There would be another patient for us to tend to and care for, another furrowed brow for us to wipe, and another person's pain and anxiety for us to ease.

A smile, a hug, and thanks from a patient or the relatives tell me time and time again that doing my job means so much to another human. Seeing members of the healthcare team, be it physicians, nurses or any other team member going the extra mile for patients or colleagues brings a warm comfort to your heart. When I am exhausted and I am just about to collapse from the sheer intensity of my job, I get a break from it all by asking one of my colleagues to take over. Apart from all the nursing skill and competency we can muster, it is these special, tender, and super awe moments that define why we do and continue to do what we do.

Strength and Fortitude Are Your Armour in Standing Tall

Live as if you were to die tomorrow.
Learn as if you were to live forever.

Mahatma Gandhi

I remember very early in the days after I graduated, I was working in a medical ward or unit. I met this amazing patient who was fighting the tough battle against cancer. He was in his early thirties, a tall lanky man. His hair had fallen off, and the chemotherapy physically affected him. The chemotherapeutic drugs in the eighties were less sophisticated and had numerous side effects. Every time he came in for a chemotherapy session, he had bad, loud retching, and his body shook with the vomiting that tormented him. We had to put him in a separate room as this affected other patients and visitors. They could not endure his suffering for long. He was a strong man and always came alone for his sessions.

Why do I mention him? Because despite his personal pain and anguish, he always made it a point to humour the nurses and the other patients. He was always smiling, and at times when he was a tad bit better in health, he came in with his guitar, and he played to all of us. He is the one who first introduced me to the concept of TLC, which is 'tender loving care', which supposedly nurses are famous for—or at least, I do hope we are famous for it. Memories of this patient have stayed with me; his peace, calmness, and happiness have touched me.

And that, my dear one, is what life is all about. Despite what life dishes out to you, smile and laugh, and the pain and the gravity of the situation will become easier to endure. If you lash out at life, if you are angry with life, you are then bitter and cranky because that is what is inside of you.

An Open Letter to My Nursing Family

Turn your wound into wisdom.

Oprah Winfrey

Though the last couple of years I have not been directly involved in nursing, in my heart I identify with being a nurse. That is my core, my identity. And I cannot wipe away the tremendous impact that the nursing field has had on me. Actually, it has been a way of life, and I wish to impart some of the values that I have imbibed from being a nurse.

First and foremost, it has taught me to be more compassionate, to not take anything in life for granted. I do know that we do have our off days, especially if we are understaffed and overworked. I know we wish at times to throw in the towel, as they say, or give it all up. Some days it all seems so futile, and the stress of the job all but envelops us.

There are days that we feel very down and depressed with all the pain that we see around us. You just have to hang in there with perseverance and determination. I know this pain can get to us; at that time, I take a breather. I have to consciously and continuously remind myself that our patients are our first priority. However difficult it was at times, I tried to smile at the person who is on the hospital bed, as he or she is incapacitated and is worse off than me. We are on the other side of the bed, connected to the bed, but not lying on it. It is also unfair if we judge our patients and their relatives.

Offer a warm touch or a cup of coffee, which has nothing to do with any competence or skills. It is not always about our nursing competence; we are called upon to care, which should be an integral part of our service, not just to provide nursing skills. We are human and sometimes seek appreciation externally through our patients and their family or relatives. I would go a step further to say that if at times you do not receive this appreciation, please appreciate yourself for the tremendous efforts that you put in, day in, day out.

We are advocates for our patients, so if you are aware that something has gone wrong, however difficult it is to discuss it, report it and communicate it. We must do what we have to. Remember, we took the oath to do no harm to our patients. Patient safety must be our focus, and we must work around this principle. We do have a tough job, and we were not promised it would be easy.

I do wish to remind my friends and colleagues to remember the Nightingale Pledge, which we had undertaken during our initiation into nursing and then probably put on a back burner, forgotten. I want to refresh you with some of its words: 'I will do all in my power to maintain and elevate the standard of my profession.' The question to ask ourselves is, do we really do all in our power to elevate the standards of nursing? So if the job asks of us to step up, then step up we must.

Before I end this open letter, I must implore to each one of you that you take the best care of yourself and your family as nursing is an integral part of the health-care industry; without nurses, health-care provision will come to a standstill.

Conclusion

In Nursing, everyday someone touches
your life or you touch someone's life.

Anonymous

We were waiting for the elevator, the slow cardiac types that are found in a hospital. I was with my sister, standing and waiting patiently for the lift to descend. A group of patients and visitors had gathered. As the lift descended and opened on our floor, we all strode inside the machine. One of the patients was carrying in her hands a newborn infant. She was asked by another as to why she was visiting the hospital. This is a conversation that we were privy to as it occurred while the elevator slowly made its way up. The lady answered that her infant baby has cried only during birth and then she had not heard any more cries from the baby; it has been about a week after the birth. Now hearing this conversation, my sister, who is a mother, was greatly upset and disturbed, and somehow she could not shake it away from her mind. And that is how the next question rose.

What makes us nurses tick?

How could we go about our duty without being disturbed emotionally? How could we appear as calm and composed at all times? Are we unfazed by all the pain around us?

I have to tell you that we do get affected by the emotional drain. Yet each one of us finds different ways to deal with the pain of what we witness daily.

We try to remain composed even when the situation is highly dramatized and emotional. When we go home after a day of work, we try not to dwell too much on the sadness and suffering. We accept that life has its grim moments. Emotional maturity comes with the job. We come out stronger, tolerant, and able to take on the world as death for us is an inevitable, guaranteed feature in our lives. Though we see so much of misery and pain, we rise above all of it as most of us see that hope reigns. We absorb the wisdom that comes out of situations and learn to heal within. Even though we get to witness deaths, we do not allow it to get us down. We accept the imminent death and help to make the grieving process easier. We feel honoured that we are present when humans come into this world as well as being part of their lives by holding their hands when they go.

We are also very perceptive, and in the hospital, we feel the love of patients' families towards our patients. In the same breath, we also feel when the patient is not cared for or unloved by their family. Many a time, there are no visits by the family, and the patient is very lonely, in pain. The physical pain of patients can be overcome, and we do help with analgesics or painkillers, but what about the emotional pain of loneliness that the patient feels for?

Stories of recovery and positive outcomes have been many, but I have not added many of them as they do not impact you as much as when pain is raw and visible for everyone to see. We reach out to touch the hands of those afflicted by pain and misery.

Why did I write this book? I felt a fervent desire to share stories of courage, faith, love, and pain. In addition to all this, I also highlighted how we in hospitals think and feel and what we endure day in, day out. Presently, I stand away from clinical bedside nursing. I do not do the hands-on any more, but the many years of nursing experience, these moments are deeply ingrained in me—though I do not touch it any more. What moulded me as a human being and as a person still touches me every now and then. I have grown a long way since then.

We make a difference, and I shall end by mentioning what I heard long ago and really do believe in. An anonymous person had rightly said, 'In Nursing, everyday someone touches your life or you touch someone's life.' I am not sure if I ever did touch anyone's life or made any impact. Yet I can tell you right now that I have been touched many times over by my patients and their families, by the people who manage hospitals tirelessly day and night, by the wonder of miracles, the power of the unseen, and the power of the invisible so close to those of us who work in hospitals that you could nearly touch and feel it many times a day.

Your joy is your sorrow unmasked. Together
they come, and when one sits alone
with you at your board, remember that
the other is asleep upon your bed.

Khalil Gibran